If You're Having A Crummy Day...
Brush Off Th

Mims Cushing

Illustrated by Greg Hettinger

**All proceeds from the sale of this book
go to The Neuropathy Association for research.**

If You're Having a Crummy Day...
Brush Off the Crumbs!

Illustrations by Greg Hettinger

Book Design by Jean Johnson

Library of Congress Control Number: 2002092048
ISBN: 0-9719400-0-2

First printing: June 2002

Second Printing: August 2002

Printed in the United States of America by
Morris Publishing
3212 East Highway 30
Kearney, Nebraska 68847
1-800-650-7888

To order copies by mail, contact
The Neuropathy Association, 1- 800-247-6968

"Pain, whether mental, physical, or emotional, robs people of sweet times. Mims Cushing's book gives insight, inspiration, and hope to those who suffer. You'll learn how to cope with stormy days and live a sunnier life."

--- **Zorba Paster,** M.D., Host of **On Your Health** and author of **The Longevity Code: Your Personal Prescription for a Longer, Sweeter Life,** soon to be a PBS Special. Clinical professor, University of Wisconsin Medical School, Madison.

"This delightful collection of personal stories will help your crummy-day crumbs magically disappear as you read them. Mims Cushing reminds us that doing the kinds of things we have always enjoyed will help take our mind off what ails us."

--- **John Senneff,** author of **Numb Toes and Aching Soles: Coping With Peripheral Neuropathy; Numb Toes and Other Woes: More on Peripheral Neuropathy,** and **Nutrients for Neuropathy.**

"This book is better than chicken soup for anyone having a crummy day.

--- **Dr. Alan Berger,** professor of Neurology, University of Florida.

Table of Contents

Foreword

Pain is one of the most common and disabling manifestations of peripheral neuropathy. It has been my experience that patients' ability to function despite pain, is in large part dependent on their attitude. I remain amazed at the diversity of patients' reactions to chronic pain and the varying degree to which patients are able to function despite severe pain. Why is it that some patients refuse to allow even severe pain to disable them, while others, with lesser pain, are completely incapacitated? My opinion is that patients' attitudes regarding their pain and what they choose to focus on go a long way in determining how they cope. In addition, patients who accept their condition, and their limitations, are usually able to function better than those who continually feel victimized. The bitterness associated with being the victim appears to exacerbate the pain, preventing the patient from being fully functional.

In many ways, the underlying difference among those who cope with pain and those who cannot is what they choose to focus on. Fortunately, the object of one's focus is under free will, although it may take great willpower and mental training. Functioning patients think, *"I know I have pain, and it's bothersome, but I need to concentrate on what I intend to do today and not let the pain interfere."*

Those who cannot function tend to think, *"Oh God, another day of pain. I can't take it."*

Any time patients focus on something other than their own pain, they go a long way to cope with their discomfort. Mental attitude and distraction often play a great role in changing a patient's focus. Successful coping involves dealing with daily setbacks and placing them in perspective. Patients who are able to accept that today is a bad day, but that tomorrow will be different, are usually the most successful in coping with their pain.

Some of the ideas illustrated in this book are perfect ways for people to distract themselves. The key is choosing what you focus on and finding what you want to become the dominant focus of your life. Some people do it naturally and they tend to be productive and happy. Others have to train their brains to change their focus. Perhaps this book can aid them in that endeavor.

Alan R. Berger M.D.
Professor of Neurology
University of Florida

The gem cannot be polished without friction, nor the man perfected without trials.
— Chinese proverb

Preface

"How do you feel, Mom?"
"I Feel LOUSY!"

I can hear her still. My mother, the funniest, wittiest, warmest, and most incredible woman I've ever met, was and is no stranger to feeling crummy. In her younger days, she'd let people know if she didn't feel well. She wouldn't hang back. Even today, at her retirement home in Rye, New York, she'll say the words in exactly the same way. Accent on the first syllable: "I Feel LOUsy!" She was 94 on St. Paddy's Day, 2002.

When I was growing up, we lived in a wonderful old brick house in Larchmont, New York, on an inlet of Long Island Sound. Winters were wicked cold and snows ran to several feet, often falling the hardest around my birthday, January 11. Snow days — no school — on the 11th were literally heaven sent. January was often known for being an "I Feel Lousy" month for Mother. And so was February. Sometimes March too. But not day after day. Just scattered days, here and there, because when Ma's back hurt or "Arthur" (her arthritis) arrived, she knew what to do. She was a master at conquering a no-good, I-feel-rotten day. And still is.

7

First You Put Your Two Feet Into Some Socks

My "Feeling Lousy" days are for a different reason: I have Peripheral Neuropathy, meaning the nerves leading to the feet (in some people, hands) have gone haywire and have decided to stay that way. In my case, the cause is unknown. If I don't take Neurontin faithfully (and sometimes even if I DO take it) I have burning, tingling, aching, numbness, sometimes stabbing pain going on in my feet and calves. Most days I deal with it by being nice to myself. I start with wearing good seamless socks.

Some days, however, my feet behave like prima donnas. I envision them fighting over which annoyance they will let be Top Dog on a particular day: *"No way! I want to do some tingling today. You let her feet burn all day yesterday."* On days when they are all fighting against one another, that's when I say, "OK. That's it. I'm having a crummy day." Usually it's because I'm stressed about something (good stress or bad), or eaten the wrong things (too many sweets), or because I did too much the day before. All this affects the Neuropathy.

I started a support group in my town, Jacksonville, in October 1999 purely for selfish reasons: there was no such local group, and I wanted to meet other people with Neuropathy. I wanted to know if there were others like me, and if there *were*, I wanted to know what they were doing about it. And that's still why people come to our

8

support group. St. Luke's Hospital said we could meet in a room off the cafeteria. In the beginning we were six, including a woman who was trudging around St. Luke's, too terminally bored to sit by her husband's bed — he was recovering from heart surgery.

In 2000 we moved to Brooks Rehab Hospital for reasons of space. At most meetings we average around 30 people. Two hundred people have stopped in over the years and have discovered they are not alone in this bizarre disease that 20 million people may possibly have.

Recently I asked the support group, "What do you do when your Neuropathy flares up? Or when you find you're having a crummy day?" Someone offered, "I lower my expectations." Not a bad idea. A few days after the meeting, I sent everyone an e-mail listing ways to conquer crummy days or make them seem more manageable. The idea for this little book sprang from that e-mail.

In The Crumbs

At the age 58 I've figured out if I fight feeling crummy and go on with my hectic schedule it takes longer to recover. Psychologists agree. This book offers ways that work for people when they're in the crumbs. Here's hoping these suggestions help you learn some ideas to keep in your pocket for future crummy days.

Whether you feel crummy from the angst of everyday living or because you're suffering from a medical or emotional difficulty, I hope you will find a bit of cheer reading the personal stories. I send my prayers and hope to all of you who, for whatever reason, need a tablespoon of honey to brighten your day. I hope the book accomplishes its mission.

Hardening of the attitudes is the most deadly disease on the face of the earth."

— Zig Ziglar

This book is dedicated ...

To my Mother. Marguerite Agathon ... Mama ... Mummy ... Ma ... Maw ... Baby Doll ... Mama Baby ... In our family, if you had a lot of nicknames you were loved. Mama, you instilled in me a love for books that won't quit. You taught me that with a book I am never alone. More importantly, you made me realize if I have myself, I am never alone. Because you kept a diary from age eight on, I did so too and now have fifty diaries, three drawers full of memories that I savor from time to time. You encouraged my writing from third grade on, even the story I wrote when I was eight, a tale about a little girl on a deserted island plotting to murder her father. (I must have been reading a *Nancy Drew*, or Dad must have forbidden me a second dessert, or both. I never finished writing that story.) Thank you for sharing your love of chicken salad on rye and the Atlantic Ocean.

To my husband, Sam. You are an amazing genius, but I simply had to turn down your suggested title for this book: *Feeling Lousy? Brush Away the Lice.* I'm only kidding when I say Charliedog is my significant other. You are my hero when the barbecue fire gets scary, the mattress needs turning, and when the cartridge in my printer dies and absolutely refuses to deal with anything resembling words unless you are around to coax it into production. You have read every article, play, and book of mine, proofread them, offered suggestions, and encouraged me to keep on writing. After all these years, you still tell me "I'll always be there for you ... HON!" And we both collapse with the giggles because we hate it when people in stores call us "Hon." I love you, Sam. Hon.

To Jay Keeshan, and to Melissa and Dave Coughlin, and their three little girls, my cherished granddaughters, Mackenzie, Kallianne, and Schuyler Coughlin: how can I not send a message of "I love you" to my son, daughter, son-in-law, and three tiny girls? Thank you, Jay and Melissa, for not griping when I wrote stories about you during your teenage years for the local paper. To all of you, be grateful for one another's love, friendship, and loyalty. Always remember, after good health, family is everything. And don't forget the yellow Post-It note on the refrigerator: "Work Hard, Behave Nicely, and Be Friendly and Helpful." (Are you groaning?) I am endlessly proud of you all.

Acknowledgments

Enormous thanks to my writing group, the River City Writers, a.k.a. *Really Creative Women*: Joan Erisman, Jean Johnson, June Lands, Claire Newkirk, and Carole Varney. I do so appreciate all of your combined efforts, combing through my stories, offering your suggestions week after week at the Green Bean Coffee House.

In particular, special huge thanks to Jean for jumping in so readily to make all the pages fit for printing. And especially for picking me up when I had meltdowns over computer problems.

Joan, your hilarious article on hunting turkeys should be in everyone's hip pocket for a crummy day. June, your thought-provoking essays about all things southern, about walking on the beach and playing around the house and garden have brought me great enjoyment. Claire, your funny stories about your trips make me want you to go on vacation — until I remember that would mean you'd be away, and that's no good. Jean, your stories about your family are brilliant; I wish I could be part of your family's "Telephone Tree." And Carole, our newest member, we have seen glimpses of some wonderful writing. We are glad you joined us.

Aren't we lucky that we love wrestling with a tangle of words every week as we write? Here's to continued great times at Green Bean, laughing together, especially over the nude calendar idea. (Who would ever think up such an outrageous thing?)

To Dr. Norman Latov, Director of the Peripheral Neuropathy Center of Cornell University, New York City, and medical advisor to The Neuropathy Association: When you read my personal essay about Neuropathy in 1999, you said, "This is marvelous! It will get published right away." I laughed and said, "Dr. Latov, I wish publishing were that easy!" Eventually, the piece found its way into The Neuropathy Association's newsletter. Dr. Latov, you told me to write a book and here it is. I am also indebted to the staff at "Neuropathy Central," New York City. I am grateful for your support, work, and confidence in this project.

In particular, thank you to Dr. Alan Berger, Professor and Associate Chairman, Department of Neurology, University of Florida, Shands Jacksonville. Without your attendance at each meeting, our support group would not be so well educated. Aside from being one of the leading doctors in the field of Neurology in the Southeast, your loyalty to the group and patience with our repetitious questions never ends.

To the wonderful people in the Jacksonville Peripheral Neuropathy Support Group: Being with you on the second Saturday of every month (except August, I know, I know) means so much to me. When the meeting has ended, I feel buoyed, my adrenaline is leaping, (Is that medically correct?) and I'm set for the day. Your personal medical stories humble me. I know you are getting solace from others. Our camaraderie is a light in the dark, and there is much darkness about this disease. Be well, and yes, I do believe the Association's motto: *Together we can beat this disease.*

And thanks also...

to Vaughan Walker and Stephanie Bugbey for volunteering to proofread this whole thing, and for doing it so promptly and with such good cheer; to the incredibly well-read Bill Dulaney, friend of mine, Friend of the Library, great proofreader and unparalleled joke teller; to Mary Policastro, for her brilliant suggestion of illustrator Greg Hettinger, who devoted many hours at college and two mornings of his spring break to draw the illustrations; to Jerry Policastro, who took a walk on a path one day and started me writing what I've chosen to be the final personal story in this book.

Part 1: Brushing Off The Crumbs

If You Do Not Have Peripheral Neuropathy, but Have Garden Variety Crummy Days ...

If You're Having a Crummy Day... would never have come to fruition without the encouragement from the people in the Jacksonville Neuropathy support group. The book started out as a list of suggestions to help us deal with days when the Neuropathy is, as someone put it, "behaving badly." Members of the group suggested that people with an assortment of other types of physical or emotional woes could benefit from a book such as this. After all, they said, *"Have you ever met anybody who can claim they've never had a rotten day?"*

The book doesn't pretend that it can help those suffering life-altering miseries. But it may offer ideas to help some people through rough days. The suggestions have not come from Ph.D's who are experts in the field of Crummy Days. The coping ideas have come from people like you and me who know what it's like to have a bum day and have figured out that a pity party is not helpful.

While physical pain may be largely responsible for down days, troublesome emotional relationships can cause them too. A psychology book called *Stop Walking on Eggshells* by Paul T. Mason and Randi Kreger (New

Harbinger Publications, 1998, $14.95) has a section called "Taking Back Control of Your Life" that includes many ways to get through days with a demanding or verbally abusive boss, friend, relative, or spouse.

Chances are good that if you do not have Peripheral Neuropathy you know someone who does — someone in your family or a friend. In fact, you probably passed someone at the mall today or saw someone walking on the street who has it.

Twenty million people have been diagnosed with Peripheral Neuropathy or have the disease but haven't been diagnosed yet. You'll see the statistic of "20,000,000 people" more than once in here, because the figure demands respect. The next section will give you some information on Peripheral Neuropathy. I hope you will take a few minutes to read it and will find it enlightening, because outside of raising money for research, a major goal of this book is to educate people about this sorely under-recognized condition.

Pain and pleasure, like light and darkness, succeed each other.
— Laurence Stern

If You Have Crummy Days Because of Peripheral Neuropathy ...

"You have peripheral what? Oh. You mean you have problems with your eyes?"

"No," I explain to my friends, "you're thinking of peripheral vision. Peripheral Neuropathy is a disease more than twenty million people in the United States suffer from but most people don't know about it."

You don't have to have Peripheral Neuropathy to have a crummy day. But if you have it, it's likely that you will be "in the crumbs" once in a while. Peripheral Neuropathy is a strange, strange disease. It comes from damage to the protective coating of the nervous system. In its informative pamphlet *Explaining Peripheral Neuropathy*, The Neuropathy Association defines it as "... the term used to describe disorders resulting from injury to the peripheral nerves. It can be caused by diseases that affect only the peripheral nerves or by conditions that affect other parts of the body as well. And symptoms almost always involve weakness, numbness, tingling, loss of balance, or pain — usually in the arms and legs."

Since autumn of 1999, we have had 200 sufferers in the Jacksonville area drop in on our support group. Some come to every meeting. Some drive two hours on a

Saturday morning to be with others who are in the same situation. Some are in such chronic pain that no painkiller can reach it. Some have chronic problems with the sensations listed above. And some people visit our group once, then realize the disease is not just "in their head"; other people have this problem, too.

Diabetic Neuropathy claims one third of the diagnosed cases. Cases can be mild or severe, resulting in amputations. On the other hand, I know a man with diabetes who can't believe people would even need a support group. His Neuropathy is mild. He is lucky. Others in the group, diabetic or not, have found their problems have escalated to the point where they need leg braces, a cane, a walker, or an electric wheelchair.

All of us in the support group have one thing in common: we're not dummies. You have to be bright and persistent if you're going to cope with this disease. Many attendees have gone to several doctors to get a diagnosis. In a third of the cases there is no known cause, a fancier word for cause unknown being "idiopathic."

Neuropathies can be acquired or inherited. Most are not genetic. Some people come to the group saying chemotherapy caused the problem, or the trauma of surgery, or other types of trauma. Specifically, there are 132 types of Neuropathy listed in the Association's *A Guide to Peripheral Neuropathies*. This list is fascinating.

Many problems you may have heard of are all included under the umbrella of Neuropathy: Lyme Disease, Leprosy, Hepatitis, Bell's Palsy, Herpes, Shingles, lead or mercury poisoning, or drug-induced problems from chemotherapy are just a few.

Here's one example of Neuropathy you surely know: Carpal Tunnel Syndrome (Entrapment Neuropathy). It's a type of mononeuropathy in which a single nerve is being compressed or squeezed. That's a more-or-less easy one to deal with, though painful. Surgery can relieve the problem. Sciatica is another example of a Compression or Entrapment Neuropathy.

Tell friends not to wait too long to see a doctor if they have foot or hand pains, numbness or weakness. They could be deficient in a vitamin or have an infection, in which case early diagnosis is so important; in some instances the Neuropathy can be reversed. If you have Peripheral Neuropathy you have to be your own health advocate. Join The Neuropathy Association.

How I "Came Down With" Peripheral Neuropathy

For me, it was exactly the way you succumb to the flu: one minute you don't have it, the next minute you do. At least that's what it seemed like; that's when I noticed it. Perhaps the weird sensations had been creeping up on me, but I didn't notice. I bought shoes at a mall in

Georgia, and the next day, wearing them without socks, my feet were tingling and burning. Wouldn't you blame the shoes? I did. So I stopped wearing them. The annoying sensation continued.

I read an article in *The Neuropathy News* about a man who searched for 25 years until a doctor figured out that he had Peripheral Neuropathy. Doctors don't say quite as often as they once did, "There is nothing that can be done. You have to live with it." That's what a respected Connecticut doctor told me. My Neuropathy is sensory, but not due to a tumor, which is sometimes the case.

There is medication for PN, but some people can't tolerate it. Many in our support group are on Neurontin, a drug whose label use is for epilepsy. But the pills can leave you feeling exhausted. The first year I was on it, I would have to (truly have to) collapse on the nearest sofa and nap for at least an hour both mornings and afternoons. When a person literally snaps asleep, is no joke. I fell sound asleep at the wheel of my car at a stoplight and "came to" only because a man rapped on my window and said, "Are you all right, lady?" Now when I'm drowsy at the wheel I pull over and nap.

Sometimes the Neurontin robs people of short-term memory, which all of us in the support group brush off with titters of "senior moment, senior moment," if we forget a name or a word. Some take 12 of these every day.

I was on eight in 1999. It took a while for me to realize my dizziness was due to the Neurontin. (My husband says I'm dizzy enough without the pills.) Three pills are enough for me now. Over my computer is a badge I picked up at the Neuropathy Get-Together in Las Vegas: "I'm Having a Neu Rotten Moment." It's amazing the things I blame on the pills. My soufflé fell? Must have been the Neurontin.

Smiling Uses Fewer Muscles Than Frowning

During the past several years, people I've never met have called to talk about their Neuropathy or have e-mailed me. What amazes me is the attitude they bring to this condition. Dr. Alan Berger confirmed that often the sickest are the most cheerful; those with the mildest chronic pain are sometimes the most gloomy. Gloom, like stress and negative attitudes, is infectious.

It's not surprising that people who do something positive with their lives cope the best. They are not letting this disease get the better of them. Some have discovered that doing something for others is really doing something for themselves. A Chinese proverb says, "A bit of fragrance always clings to the hand that gives you roses."

Sayings about positive attitudes are (positively) flourishing:

- "You can't control the things that happen to you, but you can control your attitude toward them."

25

- "If you want to see a rainbow, you have to put up with the rain."

- "No baby was born with a negative attitude. Negativity is learned, and can be unlearned."

- "Turning an obstacle to your advantage is to head toward victory."

Crummy days come in many ways. "Crummy" can happen because you feel lousy mentally, emotionally, or physically. The physical part is the easiest to understand. Your *fill-in-the-blank* is killing you, driving you crazy, hurting like blazes. No questions asked. You're entitled. The other two are more complicated. It could be that the kids are driving you nuts, the housework is overwhelming you, or a work or school project is frustrating you. It's often because of problems you're having with other people — a spouse, a relative, a work associate, or a friend.

May I Come Back as My Dog?

If we notice a plant is wilting, we give it water, sunshine, or plant food. If our children are sagging after a tough day at school, we cheer them up. If our car sputters, we get it to the shop fast. If our pets seem ill, we stroke them to make them feel better. Can't we be at least as nice to ourselves as we are to our dogs and cats? A few years back I read this variation on the Golden Rule: "Do unto ourselves as we would have others do unto us."

26

People don't treat themselves nicely enough. If you treat yourself nicely first, if you're loving and lovable to yourself, then you're ready to treat others nicely.

Burning the Midnight Oil

For those who do have PN, and for those who know someone who has it, I recommend a book that many in the more than 212 Neuropathy support groups know well: John A. Senneff's, *Numb Toes and Aching Soles: Coping With Peripheral Neuropathy* (Medpress, $22.95). He has a follow-up book: *Numb Toes and Other Woes: More on Peripheral Neuropathy,* same publisher and price. (website: www.medpress.com) You can order them through a large bookstore chain or the website.

Whether you have Peripheral Neuropathy or not, if you have a way to get yourself out of the crumbs, I hope you will write and give me your suggestions. You can send them to me c/o The Neuropathy Association, 60 East 42nd Street, Suite 942, New York, NY 10165. Or e-mail me at mims1@attbi.com.

Web sites I've found useful are www.neuropathy. com. (and also dot org) and www.neuropathy-trust.org. The last one is based in the United Kingdom and the address is Neuropathy Trust, P.O. Box 26, Nantwich Cheshire, CW5 5FP, United Kingdom. Support group member Eugene Richardson recently told me about a Trust booklet he recommends called *Peripheral Neuropathy and Neuropathy Pain Under the Spotlight* by Andrew Keen.

If you're interested in knowing about "PN" from a personal, non-medical point of view, you might find an article I wrote helpful. It's in this book (page 211), but first appeared in the December 2001 issue of *The Neuropathy News*. It's entitled "Peripheral Neuropathy: Can This Disease Be Stomped Out?" People e-mailed me from dozens of states, even Australia and Scotland. Many wrote that my experience mirrored theirs. All were pleased that attention was paid to the personal point of view, and all of them hope more attention will be focused on Peripheral Neuropathy, in magazines, TV, newspapers.

Why the Personal Stories?

For millions of people reading is a refuge. Oprah's resounding success with her book club is a good example. If you can lose yourself in a book, your pain or everyday agitation almost disappears. I've included some short personal stories written from 1994 to the present time for two reasons. One, it would be a rather small book without them, and two, maybe the little anecdotes will provide you with five minutes or more away from your crummy day. Most of them are lighthearted, but others are more reflective. On some days nostalgia may be more to your liking. In any event, I hope you enjoy them for one reason or another on sunny days or cloudy.

And one more thing: often, writing these stories helped me climb out of feeling crummy into feeling better. Along the writing path, my mind was focused not on feeling lousy, to use my mother's word, but on hunting for a better word, or paragraph, or ending. I urge you to write. Writing is therapeutic. Time flies if you enjoy it. Like anything else, you get better and better the more you practice, just like you do when you practice an instrument. The stories in *Brush Off The Crumbs* are just writings from my journals. Try journaling. Joel Saltzman titled his book: *If You Can Talk, You Can Write*. He is right.

The List

I've included the following list that I hope will jump-start your thoughts on how you can take a deep breath and say to yourself, "slow down." With luck, the suggestions will help you brush off the crumbs.

Do be sure to plan ahead. Make a list of simple pleasures that you can enjoy on a "stormy" day. Then when you're having a crummy day, look at your list and choose the right treat to bring you comfort. You know those crummy days are unavoidable, so find a space in your home where you can stash favorite books, tapes, CDs, candles, sketch pads, etc. — whatever works for you.

There is nothing so bad that good will not come of it.

— Spanish proverb

Ways To Feel Better
When You're In The Crumbs

When my feet hurt, I can't think. — Abraham Lincoln

Here's the list I mentioned earlier that I e-mailed my support group to use when they're having a difficult time. They sent back some suggestions to me, which I've listed as well. I realize ideas that are of interest to some will set others' teeth on edge. I can't see men being thrilled with the idea of a pedicure. Check off the ones you like.

If you are employed, you may find some of the ideas from this list cannot be realistically put into use during your working day. Perhaps you can keep them for when you return from work. As crummy days aren't restricted to Mondays through Fridays, I hope some of the suggestions can be tried on a weekend. Many of the ideas came from retired people. Retirees can choose widely from the list.

Solitude might be the best thing for some; on the other hand, you might need to be with many friends ... or one. Find what's right for you and start checking off or circling the things you want to do on a crummy day. And then plan ahead. If you're feeling down, you won't have the energy to do anything. Be prepared! Buy candles for a crummy day. Or paperbacks. Or tapes. And so on. Have your treats-for-a-crummy-day nearby. OR do something constructive, productive. Many choices that follow revolve around accomplishing one small task.

We're all great at sliding along happily when things are going our way. Growing older, you learn to deal with bum days. As Art Linkletter said, old age isn't for sissies. Maturity teaches us how to live gracefully with life's trouble spots. Taking time out should, however, be just that: taking a break, not using the "crummy day" excuse to sloth around for days on end.

And one last reminder: if you have Neuropathy and feel you are alone, you're not. Nearly 50,000 people have joined The Neuropathy Association. You can read the bulletin board, chat with fellow "PN'ers" and find out about support groups in your area. The website is www.neuropathy.org or write to the address at the back of the book.

The pain of the mind is worse than the pain of the body.
—Publilius Syrus

Find a Pencil and Circle Ideas That Will Help You Get Rid of Your Crummy Day

1. Take a nap. And then another one. Or at least relax, rest. And B-R-E-A-T-H-E ... S-L-O-W-L-Y

2. Read a book — new or old. Maybe a prayer book or the Bible.

3. Watch a great videotape.

4. Go to a movie.

5. Go shopping or window shopping if you enjoy it. (It can be great therapy.)

6. Listen to your favorite music.

7. Try to link up with a good friend for a meal.

8. Do a crossword puzzle.

9. Go through your recipes and toss ones you haven't used in decades.

10. Light scented candles.

11. Try aromatherapy.

12. Put on a yoga or other exercise tape.

13. Meditate ... and do deep breathing.

14. Listen to tapes of the ocean, waterfalls, rainforests, songbirds.

15. Call up a good friend or a close relative.

16. Write in (or start) a gratitude journal.

17. Write in your diary (or start one.)

18. Buy cut flowers or a plant.

19. Clean out a kitchen cabinet.

20. Throw out stale, outdated stuff in the pantry or fridge.

The sun shines brighter after a shower. ---- Yiddish Proverb

21. Polish the silver.

22. Empty out and clean a kitchen drawer.

23. Get a desk organizer. Weed out file-folder papers.

24. Toss unneeded stuff from the tops of your night tables and the drawers as well.

25. Change your sheets and sprinkle powder underneath the bottom sheet or put a sheet of fabric softener there.

26. Brush your dog or cat.

27. Go for a walk with your dog.

28. Go for a walk with yourself.

29. Put on headphones, light a fire in the fireplace, and lie down in front of it, surrounded by cushions. In

summer, go outside and listen to music or a book-on-tape.

30. Say this mantra ten times: "Stress is catching. I will avoid people who are stressed out."

31. Surf the Internet.

32. Do the e-mail thing.

33. Put on a bathrobe and lie down with a heating pad.

34. Organize a little corner of your family room.

35. Make your bedroom clutter free.

To worry about tomorrow is to be unhappy today.
— Turkish proverb

36. Throw out all your outdated spices in the kitchen.

37. Read a story on tape and send it to a grandchild.

38. Read a story to them over the phone, or have them over for a visit.

39. Make a list of things NOT to do. Head the list with No Ironing.

40. Do something nice to the plants in your house or in the garden. Use fertilizer.

41. Volunteer for an hour at the library.

42. Go to a pet store that allows you to pat the animals.

43. If you live near the ocean, watch for whales.

44. Find something decent on TV.

45. Make and freeze one dinner for the future.

46. Take a soothing bath or shower or whirlpool bath.

47. Get a pedicure or manicure.

48. Give yourself a facial.

49. Bring out your mudpack and snooze in its cement for a bit.

50. Buy a paraffin bath for your hands.

51. Get a massage.

52. Go to lunch with a friend.

53. If you're a woman, go exercise at Curves for Women.

54. Go to a gym of any kind.

55. Read Herbert Benson's *The Relaxation Response* and relax.

He who laughs — lasts.
— Norwegian proverb

56. Think up one nice thing to do for a neighbor and do it.

57. Do something "greater than yourself."

58. Volunteer to make dinner for a young mom with kids.

59. Buy a present for a person on next month's birthday list.

60. Catch up on your magazine reading.

61. Catch up on a scrapbook.

62. Work on a photograph album for your family.

63. Start a scrapbook of memorabilia from a family vacation.

64. Start writing your memoirs — one anecdote at a time.

65. Write haiku or another type of poem.

66. If you play an instrument, use it.

67. Get out a sketchbook.

68. Go to a hobby shop and look around.

69. Buy a roll of film and take artistic shots of where you live.

70. Start a health log.

Responses from the support group:

My favorite response came from **Howard Ettlinger,** who said: "Sit in front of the fridge with the door open and a knife and fork in your hands."

There were serious responses, such as the one from **Wayne Gullett,** who wrote, "In coping I read Psalm 46. The verses I hold onto are, 'The Lord is my refuge and strength. An ever-present help in times of trouble.' Then: 'Be still and know that I am God'."

That which is bitter to endure may be sweet to remember.
— Latin proverb

Eugene Richardson, who comes to our Jacksonville meetings from Fort Lauderdale, offered things that help him cope with a rough day, but he says this is different for each of us.

Eugene adds...

- Keep a pain and symptoms log daily, rating each on a scale of 1 to 10 — with 10 being the worst — to help communicate to doctors.

- Enjoy your grandchildren as a third career; teach them; be a friend to them. Lie on the floor and build crazy stuff with Legos; answer questions that pop up.

- Swim. Try pool aerobics.

- Spend time helping others with things you've learned or heard from doctors that might help someone. This gives you a purpose that otherwise you would not have in life.

Support group member **Betty Blanton** added this to our list:

- "If I get up, get dressed and put on makeup, I look in the mirror and feel better!"

Mary Heeckt, who also frequents our support group, sent in this list. She suggests ...

- ... listen to music that is inspiring. Eyna, Yanni and Charlotte Church are her favorites.

- ... draw with colored pencils.

- ... read Mattie Stepanek's *Heartsongs,* and his other books, dating back to his work at age three. The books make her "feel stupid for feeling sorry for myself."

- ... read poetry from *Falling Up* by Shel Silverstein to make you laugh — laughter is a good remedy for pain.

- ... sit in a sunroom or sunny place, take in nature, and meditate.

- ... work with a potted garden.

- ... play with a cat, or stroke it and listen to its purring.

- ... look for easy diabetic recipes on the computer or in cookbooks.

- ... draw pictures of how you feel. She writes about this miserable disease and lists reasons why it's not going to take her life away.

Jane Cook calls her suggestions a "Survival List." In 1990, she listed 48 people "the Lord sent along to pour oil on my wounds and encourage my spirit as I tried to move forward." She says her #1 way to combat a crummy day is to call a friend and arrange to do something together.

She says, "get your mind off yourself. For me, that means looking unto Jesus as author and finisher of my faith, and reaching out to others." Her list includes taking ballroom dancing for fun and exercise, taking a writers' class or a financial class, or any class that interests you; planning a cruise, working at a crisis center. Here are some of Jane's day-to-day suggestions:

- Send cards to others who need encouragement

- Simplify your life

- Eat in a food court and enjoy watching young families in action

- Borrow a grandchild and do something special together

It is better to light a candle than to curse the darkness.
— Chinese proverb

Got A While? Stockpile!
Here's A List Of Good Books

For five glorious years, in the 1990s, *The Florida Times-Union* let me write book reviews for their "Insight" section. I wrote about 90. Working under Ann Hyman, book editor, meant working for the quintessential boss. I never had a crummy day when I was reviewing books for her. She let me review whatever I wanted. I was getting paid to write the reviews, which enabled me to go out and buy MORE books, AND I was getting free books by the carload delivered to my door. My UPS guy was envious.

Dozens of just-published books arrived at my doorstep each month from ten or more well-known publishers. These books I could keep and read or not.

Let Nero Have His Grapes

I had books dangling in front of my reading glasses day and night. Furthermore, if I crossed the ditch and drove into Jacksonville, there, in Ann's little corner of *The Times-Union*, was a feast of MORE books to take home and savor!

I hated getting paid for this because I knew anything this dreamy couldn't last. I was right. One day (a really crummy day) the paper got rid of us happy book-review campers and replaced us with syndicated writers. Oh, wretched bottom line.

Luckily, I have dozens of wonderful books I've never had time to read, books that "work" to banish days that are *cloudy*. I expect my tombstone will read, "She read a lot of books." If you, too, are a bibliophile, here are some to pick up at a used bookstore, Friends of the Library book sale, or buy via the Internet.

Just Plain Delicious (But Not Plain Vanilla) Books I Have Loved and You Should Stockpile for Crummy Days

These are not brain strainers. They are off the top of my head, with some reminders from my book reviews. Don't look for industrial strength writers here. You will, however, find strong, powerful writing.

From Way Back When ...

- *A Tree Grows in Brooklyn* by Betty Smith
- *The Education of H*Y*M*A*N K*A*P*L*A*N* by Leonard Q. Ross and Leo Rosten
- *Act One* by Moss Hart
- *An American Tragedy* by Theodore Dreiser (others)
- *Cheaper by the Dozen* by Frank Gilbreth, Jr.

- *Life with Father* by Clarence Day

- *The Catcher in the Rye* by J.D. Salinger (others)

More Recently...

- *How Reading Changed My Life* by Anna Quindlen (also *Black and Blue*, others)

- *The Poisonwood Bible* by Barbara Kingsolver

- *A Map of the World* by Jane Hamilton (also *The Book of Ruth*, others)

- *Bee Season* by Myla Goldberg

- *A Year in Provence* by Peter Mayle

- *The Midwife's Tale: The Life of Martha Ballard, Based on Her Diary, 1785-1812* by Laurel Thatcher Ulrich

A few books I reviewed and loved...

- *Another Life: A Memoir of Other People* by Michael Korda (also *Country Matters: The Pleasures and Tribulations of Moving from a Big City to an Old Country Farmhouse*)

- *The Prize Winner in Defiance, Ohio: How My Mother Raised 10 Kids on 25 Words or Less* by Terry Ryan

- *Under the Tuscan Sun* by Frances Mayes (also *Bella Tuscany*)

- *The Road From Coorain* by Jill Ker Conway (also *True North*)

- *A Walk in the Woods: Rediscovering America on the Appalachian Trail* by Bill Bryson (many others)

- *American Empress: The Life and Times of Marjorie Merriweather Post* by Nancy Rubin

- *Nickel and Dimed* by Barbara Ehrenreich

- *Once in a House on Fire* by Andrea Ashworth

- *Philistines at the Hedgerow: Passion and Property in the Hamptons* by Steven Gaines

- *Slow Motion* by Dani Shapiro

- *The Tender Land* by Kathleen Finneran

- *The Perfect Storm* by Sebastian Junger

- *The Terrible Hours: The Man Behind the Most Terrible Submarine Rescue in History* by Peter Maas

- *Into Thin Air* by Jon Krakauer (also *Into the Wild*)

- *Black Dog of Fate* by Peter Balakian

- *Traveling Mercies* by Anne LaMott (also *Bird by Bird* and *Operating Instructions*)

- *The Orchid Thief* by Susan Orlean

- *The Endurance: Shackleton's Legendary Antarctic Expedition* by Caroline Alexander

- *The Professor and the Madman: A Tale of Murder, Insanity, and the Oxford English Dictionary* by Simon Winchester

- *At the Still Point* by Carol Buckley

- *My Name Escapes Me: The Diary of a Retiring Actor* by Alec Guinness

- *Riven Rock* by T. Coraghessan Boyle (also *East is East*)

- *On Writing: A Memoir of the Craft* by Stephen King

- *The Poet and the Murderer: The True Story of Literary Crime and the Art of Forgery* by Simon Worrall

Yes, these lean toward non-fiction, but that's mostly what I reviewed. Some of them are memoirs about people who overcame great obstacles. They are inspiring. Leafing through my book review binders to compile this list, I look on each book as an old friend. They are all books you may well enjoy, and perhaps you'll lose (a little) sleep staying up to read them. As the poem goes, "There is no frigate like a book to take you miles away ..."

Part II: Personal Stories And Anecdotes

Tickling The Funny Bone...

Remembering, Remembering...

Mothering, Grandmothering...

Discovering Peripheral Neuropathy: A Personal Odyssey

The Opposite Of A Crummy Day?
A Blissful One

In my college days, I spent many hours sitting in the cafeteria at Skidmore College in upstate New York, in the bleakest of midwinters. One particular morning, a bunch of us seniors lazed away over coffee and English muffins discussing the most beautiful words in the English language. "Bliss" was one of those words along with "cellar door," "willow," "mellifluous," and "silver bells." Outside the wind chill factor was 30 degrees below zero. Sleet and rain splattered against the "caf's" windows. We were in no hurry to get to class.

Now I live in Florida, and am grateful to not have a job. I'm in no hurry to deal with inside chores. As I sit by the lake, watching an occasional duck paddling across the water, I am re-struck by that word: bliss.

Children don't have any idea what bliss is. Bliss to them is a surprise treat — an ice cream cone on the way home from the supermarket, an afternoon at the movies, winning at cards or Monopoly, or building sandcastles, the anticipation of Halloween, Christmas, Easter. What they're feeling is that inner sensation of warmth and safety. And discovering that eventually tantrums, scoldings, and boredom on a rainy day will end, and a balloon is right around the corner.

But later on in life, way later on, bliss takes hold if you're lucky. Bliss is the realization of how good life is and appreciating it. "I'm so happy for you," Mother would say to me, "You appreciate things and are grateful."

How can one not feel bliss gazing over the landscape? Bliss is seeing silly Muscovy ducks waddle across the lawn, even though a poodle is carrying on, on the other side of a glass door, barking his lungs hoarse at them. "Bliss is a spiritual feeling that overcomes you when all is so right with your world that you have to step back and be awed," somebody once said. Bliss is sitting on the grass at an open-air concert with hundreds of people sharing music that restores everybody's soul.

An afternoon at the beach, reading, doing a crossword puzzle, taking a dip in a pool, listening to the power of the waves, picking out perfect shells — these things are blissful to me, perhaps because of the memories I cherish from lazy sun-drenched days of my teens.

People cry at graduations and weddings because they are remembering similar occasions in their past. Perhaps the opposite of crying is "heart-aching" — that ache of gratefulness that you feel in your heart.

My daughter called yesterday and we had one of those conversations we both relish. "Oh Mom," she said, "I can't talk about this with any of my friends... I can only tell **you** this ..." She told me how much she adores her three tiny little girls, how amazed she is at how wonderful they are, how she loves them so much, and is so very grateful she can be a stay-at-home mom. She is feeling "young-mother's bliss." It makes me misty because the bliss I feel through her has double the power: I've been there.

I listen, cluck like a contented grandmother hen, and beam a grin I hope reaches from my home in Florida to hers in Connecticut. And I tell her how happy I am that she is grateful. She knows bliss.

When The Refrigerator Got Feet

When my husband decides something in our home needs improving, he won't rest until he figures out how to do it. For example, it's bothered him for seven years that he can't easily move the refrigerator away from the wall to change its water purifier.

Today, while I was in the middle of a phone call with Debbie, he was ready to tackle the job. "I need your help — now," he said. The clarion call. I told Debbie I needed to help Sam with the refrigerator. She thought Sam needed a snack. Sam said this project wouldn't take long. Two hours and twenty minutes later the job was done.

"We," he began, (Don't wives love *we*? Isn't this *his* project?) "We need to empty out the freezer and fridge." Now, this is a job I enjoy. I usually find a treat for me, and it's therapeutic to throw out gooey lettuce and slimy hot dogs. Sam, delegating in his best *you're in the army now* voice added, "We'll need to clean the shelves too." And then he disappeared into the garage to perform work of urgent importance on his motorcycle.

He returned as I finished slamming a batch of frozen fish on the counter, willing it to become rotten. (I loathe fish if I have to cook it.) He began to inch the fridge out from the wall. Sweat and curses dripped down Sam's beard and landed on the dog, who was jockeying into position in case there was a chance of peanut butter.

"I need your foot here. Stand on this." My job was to raise the fridge by putting my heel and considerable tonnage onto a metal lever. It was a job I was well suited for — a rare opportunity to be proud of my weight. At a cocktail party, he could say, "Meet the wife. She's able to lift refrigerators with her heel."

I raised the fridge and soon realized his head was under it. If I let the lever slip, the icebox would crash onto a goodly portion of his face. How would I explain the maimed man to his children? Explaining it to *my* kids would be easy. "Another of Mom's mishaps," they'd croon to each other. But to explain it to *his* kids — that would be tricky.

I noticed a crumpled piece of paper on the counter and read the large print at the top of the page. I hollered to him so he'd hear me over the noise of the dog barking for peanut butter. "I see you bought leverage enhancers," I said, trying to sound bright. "WHAT?" he yelled. I repeated, "I SEE YOU BOUGHT LEVERAGE ENHANCERS." He shouted back, "WHAT DID YOU SAY ABOUT HAMSTERS?"

Stationed at the sink, I was having a great time squishing freezer-burned, graying fruit juice bars, lemon and raspberry, down the drain. I kept them in their wrappers and after squeezing a few bars under the hot running water, I accidentally whooshed one out of its wrapper — splat — all over the tee shirt he'd taken off and put on the counter. Combined with Sam's hamster remark, I got a fit of the giggles. "I think we ought to have a food fight," I said. It seemed appropriate. But he, the steadfast scientist, was intent on getting little feet onto the refrigerator before nightfall. A sheet of paper headed "Appliance Rollers" had a drawing of a man and woman as they adjusted a pair of these feet under a fridge. The couple was smiling. They weren't having as much fun as we were.

***

Our job is done and it's suppertime. The fridge door doesn't stay closed without pressing it shut, and the snack bin is at eye level, where the milk used to be. I'm sure I won't be able to find anything I need to make dinner. I'll look for hamsters. If I can't find any, maybe Debbie will have us over for dinner.

Me And My Buddy, Mr. Sky Marshal

I am flying to New York City from Jacksonville, Florida, sitting next to a sky marshal. I am sure he is a sky marshal. If there is an outrageous occurrence, he will save me from peril. He is asleep two minutes after takeoff. I'm dying to pat him down. I want to check out his bayonets and Uzis. I really haven't a clue what an Uzi is. I just like the sound of it. Uzi. I make a mental note to hunt down someone who might know how to describe an Uzi or could draw me a picture. I'll ask a guy in the cigar store near Harris Teeter.

If you want to know what a sky marshal looks like, he looks like Buzz Lightyear with a huge belly. Before he sat down, my sky marshal stuffed a large, black bag under his seat with great care. *Of course* there are weapons in there. Do I need more proof? I check out his watch. It is a Swiss Army watch. What other watch would an undercover sky marshal wear?

His gold ring says "married." How bummed is his wife about his new job? He's in the sky, day after day, night after night, out of touch with his lovely family: a wife who does yoga and volunteers at church, a son of 15 who plays basketball, and a daughter, 11, who just got a part in *The Nutcracker.* Is he there when his son shoots and scores? No! Is he there when his daughter, whom he calls Princess, curtsies on stage to the Drosselmeyers at the Christmas party in the opening scene? No! He's flying. He could be in the school auditorium shooting a gun in the air to show the audience how proud he is of his daughter. His kids must think he's with the Mafia because he can't tell them what he does for a living, which is essentially not a damn thing. Day after day!

I feel so sorry for him I decide to create a wee disturbance so he can have something to write on his progress reports. And maybe he'll get on MSNBC and his kids can say, "Hey look! There's my Dad!" Maybe *I* could get on MSNBC. But what kind of disturbance can I make?

A Seeing Eye dog sits a few seats behind me. Maybe I could pretend I'm allergic to it, have a seizure, and spiral out of control up and down the aisle. But if the sky marshal has to subdue me by sitting on me, he'll squash me to death, and it's not worth it. His belly is so intimidating that I back off. Who can blame him for his big belly? All that fattening airport food... no exercise. ...

He coughs. I'll offer him a cough drop and ask him in a sexy voice, "Do you have an Uzi on you?" I'll tell him sky marshals should carry retractable swords. They wouldn't have to worry about the sharp blade and when they yell "En garde!" it would let the passengers know the place was in safe hands. He could whap people into submission.

I want to wake him up and give him my copy of *The New York Times* and tell him he needs to keep his mind alert. I wonder if there are female sky marshals. I dearly hope they aren't called marshal-ettes.

I can't stand it any longer. I cough like a baby bull elephant. He stirs. Super cool, I say, "Do you fly this route often?" He tells me he does. We exchange airplanespeak for a bit, and in no time I find out he works for a company called EuroEnviroBioChemical or something. Now I'm in trouble. I'm sitting next to a man transporting evil chemicals from Florida to New York. I look around for a sky marshal.

Ma's Affair With Larry

Okay, so maybe it wasn't an affair. But in her mid-80's Mother fell in love with Larry. It happened years before Daddy died, way before he lay in the cold November ground. *Rewind.* Come to think of it, Daddy was cremated. Anyway, he loved Larry too, in his own way.

I guess you could say Daddy was still room temperature when he knew Larry. Anyway, hot or cold while Pa was still good and alive, and after he was gone, the whole family loved Larry.

If Mother and Father had not been robbed, none of us would have met him, let alone been fond of him.

***

When my parents were in their late 60's, they moved from Larchmont, New York, to Rye, just a few villages up the way. Not too many years later, on the night before Christmas Eve when they were at a party, burglars— who knows how many — came via rowboat and broke into my parents' house on Long Island Sound. My husband and I came in the front door and noticed a strong breeze coming from the dining room. "That's weird. They've left the sliding door open." It was something they would never have done. Before we looked around, Mom and Dad drove in the driveway. She would later tell the police the party was "gay like Paris" even though they didn't ask for a review, as Dad was quick to point out. "Quiet, MAA-GRET," Daddy said, pronouncing it gruffly. When he said it that way, not "Marguerite," you knew he was annoyed with her.

We stood around, dazed, as Daddy checked out the master bedroom. Drawers from their bureaus had been pulled out and thrown on the bed, and the floor was littered with sweaters and nightgowns. Dad noticed a pillowcase had been ripped off his pillow, the contents of his piggybank, gone. At this point we weren't sure if the robbers were still in the house. Livid about his piggybank, Dad ran upstairs. Seconds later, he came bounding downstairs shouting, "I HAVE NO BULLETS!" It was so unlike him not to be hollering in French; I knew he must really be upset.

The Christmas burglars stripped my parents of some of Mother's jewelry, a precious watch belonging to my great grandfather, and some of Dad's hunting rifles. The police felt my husband's and my entrance interrupted the robbery, forcing the burglars to flee. As the Christmas gifts had been quite visible, happily encircling the base of the tree like a bracelet, we were happy the thieves didn't snatch them, too. They were apparently intrigued by a small gift, neatly wrapped, about the size of a box holding a ring. They had opened it, leaving the wrapping strewn on the front hall table. Inside was a handmade piece of art by my seven-year-old niece. Poetic justice.

Because of the burglary, my parents gave up the house and moved into what my sisters and I felt was a prison, a stodgy condo, two miles away. The view of Long Island Sound and, on a good day, New York's skyline *was* beautiful, and Mother loved lying on her bed watching the sailboats glide in and out of the harbor four stories below.

When my parents first moved in, Larry, his wife Helena, and my parents became a foursome. The two couples' apartments were next to one another. They "double dated." But troubles loomed: Larry's wife had cancer.

In the late 1970s Mother and Dad helped the couple get through Helena's hideous illness, but eventually she died. My parents comforted Larry, going to restaurants as a threesome, until Dad's emphysema turned nasty. Daddy became emotionally remote and was in constant pain, needing oxygen at home. He died in 1987. Mom and Dad had been married 59 years.

It was Larry's turn to comfort Mom, and God bless him, he did so with gusto. He made her the Manhattans she loved, sharing cocktails every evening in his apartment or hers, overlooking the twinkling lights of Long Island. They ate out often, their dinners lasting two hours or more. She talked to him on the telephone constantly, something she had berated me about when I was a teenager. One day I told her, "Mom, you're talking on the phone too much." She loved it.

I felt giddy listening to her sound as though she was in the middle of her first romance. At family gatherings, puffing on her eternal Lucky Strikes — two packs a day — she began singing, to no one in particular, in her operatic contralto, "I can't give you anything but love, baby" with her arms up, Ginger Rogers style. She hadn't been radiant in ages.

Dad never cared for the arts, but Larry was a fabulous conversationalist about music, art, literature, and Venice — Mother's passions. Best of all, she and Larry shared a love for books. They read each other's collections, classics and bestsellers, and debated the meanings and pronunciations of words. The discussion about "dour" (doo-er? DOW-er?) lasted a long time. When they went to New York City, he'd buy balloons and she'd hold them as they walked along the paths of Central Park, "giggling," she told me. How can I describe how joyful it is to have your mother tell you what a wonderful time she is having, when she's in her 80's?

They must have been quite a sight, the two of them. He carved their initials in a tree in Central Park with an old Swiss Army Officer's knife, and once, Mother said, he even carved a tiny heart *in a tabletop in a restaurant in Rye!* Does a daughter scold her mother's (platonic) lover? Or did Mother fabricate the story because of the shock effect she knew it would have on her three daughters? The oldest, Audrey: "Oh for God's sake, Mother!" The middle one, Sibby: "Mother, Larry shouldn't be doing that. He needs to talk over this obsession with a counselor." Me, the baby: "Wow! That's really cool, Ma!"

One morning Mother found Larry lying dead on the floor of his apartment. Every morning he would pick up his *New York Times* to read with breakfast. That day, the paper was still in the hallway at noon. She had a key to Larry's apartment, and just as she had found her brother lying dead from a heart attack, so too did she find Larry.

She'd come to love all his children and grandchildren during their "whirlwind romance," as she called it. Earlier in the summer Larry took her to visit his whole family in Maine. It had been an enchanted time, Mother said. He talked to Mother the night before he died, having just come back from a solo trip to see his whole family. "This time, I really had a chance to get close to the grandchildren," he said.

***

Last night, I called Mother. A routine weekly call.

Mother, loud and gruff, "HAAh-low."

"Hi, Ma. It's me, Miggy."

Total change of tone: "Well, it's my Miggy!"

63

"How are ya doin', Ma?"

Her litany: "I feel LOUSY."

My litany: "Really? What's wrong?"

"Oh nothing."

"Just kind of routine to say it? Right, Ma?"

Ma, laughing: "Heh, heh, heh!"

"Do you know what day today is?"

"What do you mean?"

"It's November 17."

Mother (taking great umbrage): "Of course I know what day it is ... How could you think I wouldn't!"

Me, just in case she doesn't know: "Your anniversary. You and Dad would have been married 70 years."

"Of course, of course."

I grope for a new topic. "A few days ago I wrote a piece about Larry and you. About how he carved your initials in a table at a restaurant."

Mother (pleased, kittenish): "Well, I'm not so sure you should write about THAT! We never, *never* fooled around, you know. I wasn't that kind of a person. When we went to Italy, he was all set to share a room, but I insisted we have separate rooms, for heaven's sake. I never did anything like that."

"Ma, do you remember the discussion about dour?"

"What? Oh ... maybe ... I think he tried to do her in ... to knock her off."

"WHAT?"

"Oh that was a stupid thing to say. Stupid ... stupid ... I never said that. That was a stupid thing to say. Larry thought I was Anastasia, you know."

"No doubt, Ma."

"Ahhh, Miggy, Miggy, Miggy ... Well, you're dear to call. Come up and see me sometime."

"I will, Ma."

The Man Is A Walking Autobiography

Last Christmas I did the unthinkable: I didn't give Sam a single tee shirt with a funny saying on it. On Christmas Day he sat under the tree, aglow with anticipation. Or maybe it was the eggnog. I stood with my arms crossed over my chest and watched him unwrap the two boxes with the Bermuda shorts I'd bought him. Half of me was ready to schoolmarm him, "Sam, you have too damn many tees. This Christmas I'm giving you shorts instead, the ones that other geezers your age wear — not the ones you normally wear that barely reach your bottom." The other half of me wanted to say, "Oh Sam, I feel so bad that I didn't get you a tee shirt this year." Oh well, maybe he wouldn't care anyway.

"I think I sense some tee shirts in here," he says. He's like a ten-year-old kid about to open a Daisy BB gun, the kind that puts your eye out. *Omigod, how could I have denied him a couple of lousy tee shirts?*

Before we were married I realized I was about to become involved with his tee shirts for the rest of our lives. I married him anyway. When we moved to Florida, all his tees — maybe 100 of them — made the cut. Even his beloved boat stayed behind. Today they lie in plastic boxes that reach the ceiling in a 10-foot closet. He only keeps 15 or so in his chest of drawers. God forbid I should spirit any of them off to Goodwill.

"The Flying Pisspot" is one he's especially proud of. Also his *Far Side* and *Leave it to Beaver* ones. He has a Don Imus Autobody Express tee, a slew of others with jazz instruments, a Dizzy Gillespie one from a jazz cruise, and a bunch boasting, "Valkyrie by Honda" and "Bike World." My biker man is a walking autobiography. He has ten blue tees from yacht races. From his Sam the Bird Man phase he has several in an assortment of colors explaining that B.E.A.K.S. stands for Bird Emergency Aid and Kare Sanctuary. One tee says, "Sammy's Seafood Seven, Slightly Outta Tuna" — the name his band came up with when they played on Block Island. Others are from islands and villages near Long Island Sound. Still others sport black Labs, fish skeletons, pigs, iguanas (intended for his grandson who no longer has the reptiles), pelicans, and Escher's mazes.

In the interest of accuracy I ask if he will get down the big plastic box from the top shelf of his closet. He retrieves it. I paw through it. He's standing over me, hovering. Bank officers don't hover when people open their safe deposit boxes. He's figured out that I'm writing about his Collection and forbids me to catalog some; they are off limits. I find "Jesus Saves but Moses Invests," "Can You Find Drunken Waldo?" and "Spirit of Billy Bowlegs Pirate Festival, Fort Walton, Florida."

Dozens are from Aruba. Each time we visit that island he buys three for the unbeatable price of $10. The fact that they instantly become tissue paper after they've done time in the washer is of no import. Dryers are strictly out of bounds. He's besotted with the flimsy shirts. He says his purchase helps the Aruban economy. Seventeen Aruba vacations times three tees means 51 tee shirts all emblazoned with sailboats and seagulls, proclaiming "ARUBA" or "ARUBA'S FLAG DAY." (Our timeshare coincides with the country's National Day.) I counter his shirt purchases by buying gobs of makeup at the airport on departure day. Estee Lauder does not sell anything "Three for $10."

Years ago, when we married, we gave tees to each other. I don't remember what I gave him, but he gave me a tee saying "My Next Husband Will Be Normal." Years later, when I played in a bellringing choir, he found shirts with funny characters attempting to be bellringers. My shirts have somehow disappeared.

Are fewer people wearing tees with punchy sayings? I think so. On the other hand, dozens of tees are in stores and catalogs. Lots of them discuss beer. "Beer is proof that God loves us and wants us to be happy." "Got Beer?" has been followed by a toddler's "Got Milk?"

There's "Knee Jerk Moderate," "Still Plays With Cars," "Power Corrupts But Absolute Power is Kinda Neat." Even father and son tees: "The Old Block" and "Chip Off the Old Block." And this incredibly long one: "If a man speaks in the forest and no woman is there to hear him, is he still wrong?" I find "Women Want Me; Fish Fear Me" bizarre.

Little kiddies have plain white tees proclaiming "Warning — I am Two." For trust fund babies, "Got Any Money for My College Fund?" The golden oldies have "When did my wild oats turn into shredded wheat?" and "Over what hill? Where? I don't remember any hill." College graduates can wear "Well-educated but broke."

On his birthday, a month and a half after my heartless Christmas offering, I caved. I bought him a tee shirt. Sam is happy again, biking over the Ponte Vedra terrain in his latest shirt, announcing "Make Noise, Do Wheelies, Leave Donuts, Be Speeding" He and his motorcycle love this shirt.

There's another reason why Sam is pleased. After his birthday dinner, when we strolled up St. George's Street in St. Augustine, he found a store selling "TEE SHIRTS —

3 for $10." They were emblazoned with boats and seagulls and "St. Augustine" written all over them.

Gravity Is Getting To Me

"Lift, lift, lift."

I'll bet a small aneurysm is forming deep inside my head, and soon the brains I have lovingly nurtured for half a century will implode like the Seattle Super Dome. Or perhaps selected pieces of brain matter will splat on the walls and ceilings to live on in perpetuity, all over the gym's interior. I suppose I could put the brakes on all this activity by breathing.

"Lift, lift, lift," she says. And then, with great cheer, "Eight more."

You'd think lying on the floor would make it easy. But with one leg up in the air, I look like a dog begging to have his belly scratched. I want to curl up in a fetal position.

But last week Barbie made us get into a fetal position, and then, damnation — she found something to make us burn our trilaterals or quadri-trisomethings. A fetal position is my coziest sleep position. Cozy is not the operative word in this class. Barbie's goal is to make us feel the pain. She's doing a good job.

When Claire told me about the class I thought I'd give it a chance. "Oh Mims, you won't believe what a difference it'll make. You'll tone up, firm up. Your waist will be smaller than it should be." That sounded good. When my sister was engaged, she told me her fiancé could encircle her waist with his hands. I don't think my mother could put her hands around my waist when I was born.

"Now pulse three times. Eight more." In a swim-aerobics class I took last week the instructor must have told us, "Good job!" every 30 seconds. I wasn't doing a good job. Barbie does not tell us we are doing a good job. Maybe she *DID* say it before I joined the class, but being a purist, and watching my foul performance, she cannot bring herself to utter, "Good work" when I'm only doing 10 pushups to everyone else's 90.

"Now turn over." I don't like being told to turn over. I feel like a hamburger. I want to eat a hamburger. Eight more and eight more and eight more. I begin to loathe the number eight. Fear it. I stare at the mirror and wonder why I'm settled in position in front of a mirror. Why can't mirrors in gyms be like carnival mirrors? Part of the wall could be glassed in so oversized people would look tall and lanky and another part of the glass would make little folks look big, for those few who are trying to bulk up.

Maybe I should breathe so the budding aneurysm will go away. On the other hand if I don't breathe I will pass out or die, and then I can stop these horrid exercises. Maybe there's a cart in the corner for people who have died here. Barbie, Dot, Claire, and Nate unceremoniously take a leg, an arm and the rest of me, and hoist my bodily baggage into a wheelbarrow.

Here's the scenario: the concierge at the club across the street is summoned to wheel me across Ponte Vedra Boulevard and dump me into the ocean on an outgoing tide. Disgusted, the rest of the group presses on with the exercises. Seaside, with a bugle blowing mournfully, I succumb to a final blast of humiliation as the concierge summons the umbrella guy, to help heave-ho me out of the wheelbarrow. I wonder if this news will make it into the club's monthly newsletter. I hope no one tells my husband about it.

What heinous crime have I committed that I must work out once a week for an hour in a class called "Gentle BodyWorking"? Is God punishing me because I killed one too many house spiders? Did I run over a squirrel? But God didn't make me sign up for the class, Claire did.

73

The class is over. I don't feel like a hamburger any more. I am a strand of over-cooked spaghetti. Claire, who is the soul of tact, eager to be enthusiastic, senses my wobbly arms and legs. "Well, the class is hard for walkers. You walk a lot and walking uses different muscles than the ones we use in class." Of course! That's it! I will stop walking and give my muscles a rest for a couple of years. In 2009 I'll think about rejoining the group. By then exercise classes might be held in anti-gravity machines. The atmosphere will automatically lift your leg up, up, up and away to a count of eight. One hundred times.

I hope Claire won't be mad at me for dropping the class. And then I think, nah. We can go to foreign movies together. And we'll practice abdominal crunches right in Pablo Theater. And buy tubs of popcorn.

"Always a Daughter, Now Too a Friend"

I lie in bed in my son-in-law's and daughter's home in Tampa, a home they moved into six weeks ago. It is my first visit. It's strange to be in their home. Am I a guest?

It's 9:00 A.M. Sun streaming in, mockingbirds singing, gentle trickling of water from the pool fountain. Then I hear a funny sound. A lawn mower? It's not the right day for the lawn guy. It's a motor, but not a car. Melissa's husband has long since taken the car to work.

The baby, Mackenzie, is sleeping, so Melissa must be too. The baby's sleeping habits rob me of the right to smirk. "Wait'll you have your own kid," I used to say, when my daughter slept till noon all summer during college vacation. "You'll have to get up at the crack of dawn then, good buddy." But she produced a baby who often arises at 10:00 A.M. Mackenzie is practicing her sleeping-late skills for college, a mere sixteen years from now.

And then I figure it out. The noise I'm hearing is a vacuum cleaner. My daughter is vacuuming? It's been humming for 20 minutes. I think terrible thoughts. She and Dave had a huge fight and she's getting her aggressions out by vacuuming. What should I do?

75

Confront her and say, "What is it, sweetheart?" But I'm learning to behave differently now that my children are adults. When they're kids, it's what you *say* that's important. When they're adults, it's what you *don't* say.

Then I realize she's vacuuming because she and Dave had a party the night before and the house needs it. I'm impressed. I bounce out of bed, shower hastily, and go downstairs, feeling guilty that I haven't wiped down all the shower tiles with a special spray my daughter discovered at Publix. She does it every day! My once-rebellious teen is Mrs. Clean. Furthermore, she tells me about grocery sales before I know about them. And raves about a special margarine made with yogurt.

If she has made breakfast for me, I will *really* be upset. I don't want to be thought of as a guest. "Hi Mom!" She is chirping. Everything is go for a good day. I happily fix my own cereal.

After the baby has been fed, another thing stuns me. She removes the tray from the baby's high chair and douses the whole thing under the faucet in warm sudsy water. (I didn't see a spot on it.) She cleans the whole chair and gets down on her hands and knees to swab the floor after every meal. She will not use a sponge because "It's unsanitary," and goes through a jumbo roll of paper towels every two days to clean the kitchen surfaces. Whose daughter is this?

Once when she babysat she reported to me that the mother made her little girls get down on their hands and knees to clean the floor from the dining room table to the kitchen sink! Will she make her offspring do this?

Melissa verbalizes something I, too, have been feeling. She says she sometimes feels that this is my house, not hers and Dave's, and that she's the kid in it. It's not dissimilar to the house she grew up in. Sometimes, when I sit and read the paper at her kitchen table, I feel it's my house, too. It's unsettling, until I remember she told me she felt the baby was mine, not hers, during the first few weeks after she gave birth. I also felt Mackenzie was my baby. We've gotten over that. She commented, "We've gotten so mature, Mom. Haven't we?"

***

Today is Valentine's Day, and Dave gave Melissa a bike. With the baby seat, they can ride around, to "work the neighborhood," i.e., meet their neighbors. Stephanie invited them to go to a swinging place in Ybor City with three other couples, for dinner and then on to a special place. "I'll have you dancing on the bar, you better believe it!" Stephanie said.

I knew it would be a late night for them, and I was happy to have the baby all to myself. By 11:00 P.M., Mackenzie was asleep and so was I. Hours later, from a deep sleep, I heard a loud banging on the front door. It was 2:00 A.M. I peeked over the banister and saw Dave and Melissa waving through the glass panel at the front door. They said they'd forgotten the front door handle had broken off and that's why they couldn't get in. They told me the evening had been fabulous, and that, indeed, everyone had danced on the bar.

I never remember being happy during their college days when they'd arrive home in the early morning hours. How happy I was, now, to see them frisk about with friends and leave the cares of parenthood behind.

The next morning the baby decided to wake up at 5:30 in the morning. The parents slept like college kids. Until noon. And nobody vacuumed.

I'm Bleeding But I Can Get Up

Last night I took a slice off my index finger. Putting down the carving knife, I grabbed handy bandages of paper toweling, wrapped up my finger several times, and went on hacking my leftover Thanksgiving ham so it could be gulped down by the Disposall.

It wasn't a big ham, but it was rotting enough to be rid of, to stuff down the sink's eating machinery, one of the few mechanical devices I've mastered along with the toaster oven, the mashed potato beater thing, and the bread baking machine (though I still can't deal with the "add nuts or raisins" part).

It was done. The ham was history. I opened the peanut butter jar and made a sandwich using two saltines, then gingerly unwrapped the Bounty-swaddled finger. Well, Lordy me. What have we here! A scenic involuntary bloodletting. A still-gushing sliced finger with a need for ice to staunch the flow. Every time I pressed more paper towel on it, a small geyser erupted.

I've been doing pretty well on my own since Sam's been traveling to visit his kids in Connecticut. I haven't called my neighbor over for any rescues. Last night I called Sam and said, "I haven't set the house on fire."

"You will," he said, with a *ha ha ha* in his voice.

The geyser continued. I went into the bathroom and whipped out the triple antibiotic. I'm in awe of that tube. Imagine the power. One pinkie-finger-sized tube can stave off an infection that can kill you. I slathered a goodly dollop of the creamy stuff onto the war zone raging on my index finger. It looked like Kandahar in Technicolor. Blood and cream mingled to produce the most beautiful frosting you can imagine. I hated to cover it over with a Band-Aid, such was its loveliness.

I used a butterfly Band-Aid, which is supposed to squeeze the cut together so the skin doesn't pull apart in the healing process. Unfortunately, I put the Band-Aid on in the wrong direction, meaning the cut will forever pull in the wrong direction.

It's amazing what time spent without a husband can do. Lately I rediscovered the power of a vacuum to make one's house look decent. When I had surgery in 1993, the surgeon told my husband he would have to take over the vacuuming. Bless him, the doctor didn't say, "for a while." Consequently, good old Sammy thought he'd have to vacuum for the rest of our lives. Last week, the vacuum started smoking as I waltzed my way around the living room. If he'd been home, I would have run screaming to him with the news. This time, I went to the Sears Factory Repair Shop and bought a new replacement belt.

Mackenzie Medals Herself

On a crisp fall morning, before Mackenzie left for preschool, she medalled herself. "Mackenzie, are you wearing that medal to school?" her mother asked, amused, when the four-year-old came to breakfast. It was a big, round, yellow, plastic disk. "Yep. I am. I want aaaall my friends to know I can ride a two-wheeler."

The excitement about Mackenzie's milestone quickly made it to the far reaches of little Miles Road on the afternoon of the big event. The street is a block of 30 families abrim with children. A fire truck from the Darien firehouse comes blazing up the street every year on Christmas Eve when it's good and dark. Santa ho ho ho's over the blasting sirens, and then stops in the very middle of the horseshoe-shaped street and hands out gifts wrapped and brought by elves to the firehouse ahead of time, for each one of the dozens of children. He looks at each present thoughtfully to find out the name and calls it out. Then he explains he must hurry off because he has a busy night ahead. Can you imagine the excitement?

Anyway, on the afternoon Mackenzie learned how to ride a two-wheeler, no one expected it would happen so fast. Her Mom unhooked her training wheels and held her seat while she wobbled away from her driveway over to her friend Mary's house next door. "You'll get the hang of it," her mom said. Mackenzie abandoned the bike and became involved with her sister Kallianne's chalk squiggles in the driveway, and then Mary's mom volunteered to take Mackenzie for another try.

Kenzie climbed on, got a push — and, to everyone's amazement, whoosh! She was off! Another few times and she was turning around! Another few times and she was flying down the driveway! Only a couple of spills. No tears. No Band-Aids. It denied her father, on a rare business trip, the pleasure of teaching her how to bike, but that's okay because his two other daughters are waiting in the wings for him to teach.

Children came around for high five's. Dads driving home from work slowed down to comment that the little girl would be learning how to drive before long. Moms with strollers shouted praise. Kallie, the middle sister, was awestruck and clapped harder than anyone at each sortie.

That night Mackenzie lay in bed, smelling fresh and sweet from her long, hot shower. Her mom finished the ritual book-reading session, then Mackenzie popped up. "Mama, help me spell something." A pad and pencil in the bedside table, ready for emergency writing sessions, was produced. "How do you spell 'Today I unhooked my training wheels'"? Laboriously, Mama spelled and Kenzie wrote. "I'm writing this in case I forget in the morning," she said.

I think grown-ups should have medals to use at their discretion. Every time you do something you're proud of, you medal yourself. You could share your excitement with people at the supermarket, hairdresser, church, the beach. People would ask, "Why the medal?" And the response would be "because today I learned how to use a complicated camera ... I learned how to mow the lawn so it doesn't look raggedy ... I spoke in front of a group without panicking ... I played handbells at church and didn't miss a note." You could wear the medal all day long. Think how great you'd feel that day. Congratulating yourself is nice, but sharing the news is fabulous. Kenzie knows this.

Why Don't We Have An Estate Sale?

They called themselves The Good Riddance Girls and they were as hard as a couple of Idaho potatoes. Cows smile more than they did. "Throw out nothing," they said. And they were right. They took charge of one estate sale each weekend and knew what people wanted. "Think your used socks and hankies aren't somebody else's treasures? Ha! People will even buy used bars of soap."

Estate sale sounded to me as though heirs were washing their hands of dead relatives' stuff: ivory cameos and sterling silver place settings for 24. Estate sale can also mean people are moving, which has a brave and romantic sound. But now that *we* were really moving, I wasn't brave at all. And not particularly romantic.

My husband, Sam, had wanted to move to Florida since the days when he visited his parents in Jupiter every winter for 25 years. When his mother moved near Jacksonville Beach in 1992, he visited her and called me right away. "You gotta see this place. This is it." We *had* been looking up and down the eastern seaboard with an eye toward moving sometime, but I was just playing a game. I thought those trips were excuses to take a vacation. I never thought we'd really move.

Scientists have legitimized the winter blues by calling it Seasonal Affective Disorder. Sam was convinced he had it. I couldn't bear to see him so down, winter after freezing winter in Connecticut. He had gotten me at a weak moment. I was so overwhelmed at work that moving to Florida seemed delicious. "Oh yes!" I said. "Get me out of this job!" All it took was one trip to Florida, and then, by God, we were *moving*. Be careful what you dream ...

That summer, Sunday after Sunday, clusters of Connecticut and New York relatives — my husband's grandchildren and grown children, my sister, my niece, her kids, my mother and her sister, and my own children — flocked to swim one last time in our pool. I went through the motions of serving chips and salsa, and chicken salad, brownies, and Margaritas. Sometimes during the sultry summer afternoons, I'd go upstairs, lie down on the bed, and sob. But people never knew. Ten minutes later I'd come back downstairs. "Anyone want watermelon?" My sunglasses were never far from my side, from June through August.

The flurry of goodbyes and parties at work had been sweet. Now, with the sale looming, reality was frightening. Moving from a house I'd lived in for 22 years ... two babies, two miscarriages, various surgeries ... the kids' prom nights and teenage heartbreaks ... sometimes frightening revelations ... a remarriage. The memories of cherished times overwhelmed me every time I walked the dog up our steep driveway and onto Bayberrie Drive. Buying the house in Connecticut had been a fairy tale. What would it be like to leave it? Once, my husband noticed how upset I was. "I can see how hard this is on you by the way you walk the dog." I asked him what he meant. He said I had never walked Amos with my head down before. Sam couldn't help with this sale. He was turning his insurance agency over to his partner. The two of them had jointly owned it for 25 years. And then there was his boat. If he's willing to part with his beloved Dagny, his beautiful sailboat, he must really be serious about starting a new life.

I wasn't thrilled that The Good Riddance Girls would get a percentage from the sale, but I couldn't handle it on my own. Two years before, Sam and I had held a little garage sale. When people said, "How about $5 for that?" pointing to a paperweight I'd tagged for $15, I caved. You want my sweet little bunny rabbit paperweight? Of course you can have it for $5!

The Good Riddance Girls would price, then tag, then sell everything. Where I might price things too low, they would not. I had no clue how to value half the stuff. Why, I might even come out better in the end. I would have dumped bottles of spices, probably twelve years old, from my spice rack, and half-used perfume bottles off the top of my dresser. "Don't!" they told me.

The day the Girls, Margaret and Lynne, walked through the house and toted up the money they'd be making from our possessions, cash registers kaa-chinged behind their eyeballs. I, myself, started feeling a little better. I'd have money to buy new furniture! I decided if you make a new start in Florida you need to buy new. You need a Florida feeling. Get wicker. Get pastels. Get light color. Get lightweight stuff you can easily move in case of a hurricane.

"You don't need to be here on the day of the sale," Margaret said, meaning, get the heck out of your house for the day. Suddenly I had little to do. One morning, just for fun, I drove all the way up to Westport to look at Country Curtains, a new store with such a New England feel to it that I cried the half an hour it took to drive home. Is everybody this unhappy when they move? No, I told myself. No, they weren't. So I bought a condo, in Stamford, Connecticut. I didn't mean to do it.

What happened was that my daughter and I were hunting for an apartment for her to rent. She graduated in June, and was starting a new job in the fall. The broker showed us places for sale or rent. Prices skyrocketed in the 1980s, but now in the early '90s condos were half their former price, or less. Melissa finally chose a nice rental, but one place we saw that she didn't like (10th floor — too high, she said) stayed in my mind. It was in the same zip code as my soon-to-be former house. At one end of the living room was a picture window with a distant view of the Sound from Manhattan to eastern Long Island. It could be my summer refuge. Sam, being lizard-like, adores the heat. He would stay South in summers.

"You are absolutely out of your mind," Sam said. "I know you'll get it, but I don't want anything to do with it." As I said, he was preoccupied with selling his boat. My New England relatives were so excited they bounced to the sky along with the 4th of July fireworks. The condo meant I'd come up north and see them.

Houston, we have a problem: On July 5th I closed on the little apartment that had dried my tears. The Girls, however, were rubbing their greedy hands awaiting the sale, July 31st. We had walked around the house together in June, and I pointed out things that could be sold. But now I needed to furnish my apartment. And with what better stuff than my cozy old La-Z-Boy? And my sofa? And I'll need pots and pans ... And I might as well bring a couple of spices ... "We won't handle a sale unless we feel it will bring in a certain amount of money," said one of the Girls when I told her Melissa was taking much of the stuff with her and I was taking a ton with me. Even more stuff I'd sent into storage for my son, Jay.

They were backing out of handling the sale! Oh bother. I had become eager to see dusty trinkets, knick-knacks, and books carted off while I was shopping at the mall. So I begged. "Oh, but we have lots of stuff I haven't shown you in the basement." They agreed.

The basement. Surely there was stuff in the basement. Yes! Sam's stuff. If he was making me move to Florida he would have to agree to get rid of the stuff that had bugged me for 11 years. "Frankly," he said, "I don't care any more. I just don't give a damn. You can get rid of anything you want." Incredible. What a dangerous thing to tell a chronic thrower-outer. Finally, via this sale, we could do away with the gigantic painting in the huge crate that neither of us had ever seen. It had been handed down unopened for generations.

He helped me uncrate it — it was six feet by three, and inside was a lead-weight, gold-leaf frame showing off a truly awful-looking relative of his. Melissa and I labeled her Aunt Hortense. It dated back to the late 1800s, black background, brown dress...very unFlorida. Save Hortense for the sale. Other small paintings, similarly dreary. Save them. Navajo rugs. Save. I was in dance mode. *Heaven. I'm in Heaven.* Sam's 25-year collection of Smithsonian magazines. Sale! Sale! Sale! I was going to get cash money for it. And it would help offset the cost of my newest child, the condo on Strawberry Hill Avenue, only six minutes away. 06902.

In the weeks leading up to the sale I'd envisioned myself offering cookies and lemonade to the buyers as I showed them the pictures of my children on the piano. I must have been out of my mind.

Three days before the sale, Sam became so glum he took up permanent residence on his boat. "It's transitional," my friends said, "Husbands get that way before a move." The Girls came to price and tag everything. The long distance movers came to take box after box of photos and memorabilia to Florida, teenagers came to move Melissa's stuff, and local movers took stuff to my apartment. Melissa found more to keep safely in storage for her brother, who was in Europe. Incredibly, the place still looked furnished.

On the day of the sale, we left the house at 6:00 o' clock. to celebrate and ate a gala breakfast at a diner. Sam had rallied. We arrived back at the house an hour later, thinking we'd look over the place one last time before the big event. Two large vans were camped in front of our house. By 8:00 A.M., a line of people formed up our brick walkway, and snaked neatly along my rhodies and day lilies. License plates said Vermont, New York.

The Girls had advertised widely, as they knew collectors might be interested in a couple of our paintings by a Vermont artist named Blodgett. No one waiting to go into the house to find "treasures" knew we were the homeowners. "Looks like the house needs a paint job," someone said, looking at our shutters. It was time for us to leave. Sam stayed at the condo to handle calls from the Girls asking for our permission to lower prices. My sister and I went to the Stamford Town Center.

Later, I found out we sold the six Blodgetts right off the walls, a tea service, and an oval portrait from the basement in the first five minutes. A couple from Greenwich was delighted to take Aunt Hortense into their bosom, to palm her off as one of theirs. In the afternoon Sam got a call from the Girls asking if we'd sell the stately Boesendorfer piano for $5,000, a steal. Sam said yes, but it broke his heart to sell it at any price. It was a concert grand and wouldn't fit in our Florida home. When Sam's heart breaks, somehow it's far worse than when mine does, because his rarely does, but mine breaks for a variety of reasons great and small. Sad movies...sad commercials. ...

Mucking about with my sister was an excellent way to spend the day. We shopped, we lunched, we tea'd, and a little before four o' clock, we headed to my house. The sale was to end soon. As we drove up the hill to our street, neighbors were standing on their lawns, looking in the direction of our house. Something, Miss Clavell would have said, was not right.

Turning onto our street, we saw a police car in front of our house. The front hood of someone's car had turned into an accordion. Somehow, it had smashed full bore into a huge oak tree on our front lawn. There were tire marks … and a huge gash in the tree. (We were to close on our house in two days. How do you repair a tree in 48-hours?)

Apparently, ten minutes before the end of the sale, a man had bought so much stuff that he'd moved his car seat all the way forward to fit his stuff in the back. Because of that, he couldn't get his foot from the accelerator to the brake. A piece of furniture fell on him from the back seat; he got disoriented and mashed on the accelerator by mistake.

His car had been in our driveway, facing the road. He had managed to propel his car across the street, up onto the neighbor's lawn facing our house. The car spun around 180 degrees, and headed full-speed into our tree. His wife, in the front seat, was holding on to a large window fan, and, from the impact against her face, had a nasty wound. When they got her out of the car they led her, bleeding massively from her forehead, into our family room. The driver was dazed.

Of course I called Sam who came over right away. I don't remember ever being so grateful to be married to an "insurance man," even though nobody sued anybody. In the end, the couple was all right. The straggling buyers were in no hurry to stop shopping. The Girls proudly announced that the cashiers, when they heard the explosion of the car hitting the tree, "had the presence of mind to take the cash boxes with them."

The next afternoon, a good friend asked if I wanted company at my pool. "Bring chairs," I said. "Mine are all gone." I had spent all morning bagging flotsam for the Goodwill guys who carted off clothes, a big rocker, a cogwheel table, and an embarrassment of a couch in the basement. Sam was sailing. He came home around six, just before the guy who bought the piano was supposed to pick it up. Sam left minutes after he arrived. It was too hard to watch the piano walk out the door. Besides, he'd found somebody interested in his boat. I was so exhausted I dragged myself through the empty, hollow rooms one last time. As a souvenir, I took the pool thermometer, even though I didn't have a pool in Florida.

POSTSCRIPT: It's ten years later. I let myself have too many crummy days that summer. I'm glad I've met so many people who have taught me how to survive days in the crumbs. If I should ever have to move again, I've got my list to see me through it.

Sleeping Beauty
Was One Smart Cookie

Remember the old advertisement with the baby crying, "I WANT MY MAYPO!" Well, I want my horse urine, the synthetic hormone so widely used and yet under such scrutiny lately.

In April, I was taking my aqua aerobics class — and by the way, why do people *take* classes? Where are they taking them? Anyway we were, as usual, driving the instructor crazy with our banter. Sometimes there are 20 of us and after a weekend we gab for the whole hour. That Monday, the topic was estrogen. Many in the class had discovered The Saliva Test. It sounds gross, but you spit and spit into a plastic jar. You need about ¼ of a cup and that means killing half an hour, seriously spitting. You send the resulting swill to a lab in its vial, and six weeks later you find out how inadequate (deficient) you are in all the hormones that keep you female.

Then the doctor prescribes natural hormones for you. Everyone seemed to be thrilled.

"I have so much more energy."

"My skin feels so much smoother."

"I sleep so much better."

"Warren and I have never had such great sex."

I debated asking if I could borrow Warren for a week, but I didn't think that's where I was meant to go. Good sex is not worth being banned from swim aerobics.

I'm a sucker for anything new that people rave about. So one morning I found myself holding a bestseller with one hand (to keep from being bored) and a spit vial in the other, hoping I wouldn't become absent minded and spit into the book.

Several weeks later, my doctor called me into his office. She said I should use a patch, which I'd need to alternate to different sites. I'd also need seven sublingual drops (7), and a cream (progesterone).

Suddenly, my simple, once-a-day pill disappeared. I'd now have to *think* about my hormone treatment. The worst was the cream, a quarter of a teaspoon, morning and night. The instructions listed nine specific sites on which I was to use this stuff: left inner arm, then right arm, left bosom, then right bosom, left leg, right leg, and chest, abdomen, throat. I can barely remember to take the dog out to pee, much less remember this routine. The jar of cream costs a fortune, and the pharmacy says everybody uses up the jar in a month's time. Wouldn't you think that, for example, a 260-pound woman should be told to use a tablespoon of the stuff and a 100-pound sylph should use the 1/4 teaspoon? Tell me how everyone, big or small, can use up a jar in one month? Go figure. Anyway, after I'd used it up in 30 days, a woman at the pool told me she used a jar about every six months! Just what I needed — another competitive venue.

Here's the thing: when I am standing in front of my bathroom sink, massaging this quarter of a teaspoon into my ample bosom, I wonder when a scientist will come up with a cream that works once a month. You smear a cup onto your entire body, wrap yourself in plastic for twenty-four hours and you're done for thirty days. Like Sleeping Beauty, I will fall asleep and wake up when my dog starts licking the stuff off me. You do remember that story, don't you? Oh gross. I want my horse urine back.

Jay, Melissa,
And A Bat Nightmare

On a still, moonless night, around midnight, a bat flew into the bedroom window of my Connecticut condo. Melissa was in the room when it happened. I was in Florida. (YESS!!) She, her husband Dave, and their 18-month-old baby, Mackenzie, had been staying there for a week. Dave had just flown back down to their home in Florida for work. My son Jay happened to be staying in the apartment that night. Thank goodness. It was good that a sturdy brother was around to save his sister from the beast.

Apparently Melissa had just gone to bed when she heard a whooshing. She thought it was the wind, but something made her snap on the light anyway. The bat was "doing laps" as she put it, over her head, swooping near her face, mustering up speed, she said, "to take a bite out of my throat."

She slid out of bed, ducked, and made it to the hall. Remembering to close the door was easy. Waking up her 29-year-old brother was another story.

"Jay?"

"Hmm."

She shook him. "Get up. There's a bat in Mom's bedroom."

She pleaded, "Really there is, Jay."

Jay, groggily: "Mel, it's just a beanie baby. Go to sleep."

Having been a good brother for almost three decades, he knew he'd eventually have to take a look. After all, he'd just gotten his Master's in Business Administration. First in his class. He could handle this. He opened the door.

"HOLY ... !!!" He estimated each wing to be a good six inches. Unfortunately, MBA or not, Jay did not close the bedroom door in time. The bat escaped to flap its flappers in the living room, making numerous passes over baby Mackenzie, a juicy sleeping target. Was the bat sturdy enough to pick up Mackenzie and fly off with her?

Growing up, Melissa always did attract critters. Her brother just laughed at her while I HIIIEEEE-YAAAA'd creepy crawlies to death. Her bedroom when she was a child was called The Spider Room. When she wanted to shower, she'd find a thousand-legger in the tub. As an adult living in Tampa, she spied a huge black snake SSS'ing its way across her front walk. Sugar ants marched in formation across Mackenzie's bedroom floor, and good old palmetto bugs bivouacked in the kitchen. The owners of Tampa pest control companies were taking all-expense-paid trips to Vegas because of their critters..

Dealing with a bat was new. Now that the "beanie baby" was in the living room, baby Mackenzie needed to be maneuvered to safer territory. She and Melissa snuggled for a while in Jay's bed, door closed. Mackenzie was a big comfort to her mother, three-months pregnant.

For most of the night Jay, later joined by Melissa, upended furniture and moved books trying to find the bat. Melissa searched with her eyes closed. Finally they checked the window screens in the master bedroom. For some reason the screen was down, an inch from the top. It's a wonder there weren't a dozen bats in the apartment.

At one point they spied a round, blackish ball in the corner. Was the bat playing possum? The "bat" was motionless for a good reason. When they stopped clutching each other the posse saw it was only a bit of potpourri that had escaped from a bowl.

Around 3:00 in the morning they called it quits and got ready to bunk together in the king-sized bed. Jay crept out of the bedroom to visit the bathroom one last time. The bat made a pass at his forehead. The creature was making our condo his motel. Jay's scream woke the baby.

Next morning, Jay found bat droppings in the living room. (More potpourri?) He vacuumed, then called the Stamford Humane Society who said it would only be worrisome rabies-wise if the bat were on the move by day. An exterminator said he could come with whiffle bats and tennis racquets, but he said the best idea was to wait till dusk, open the window, and let it fly out.

That was the plan. Melissa and the babe settled themselves at Mel's sister-in-law's house. Jay waited till twilight, set up his camp trunk on the catwalk, and sat on it. He stared into the apartment, hoping to watch the bat glissando out a window. People passing by to go to their apartments looked at him with narrowed eyes. He called me on his cell phone to pass the time. "People must think I'm a peeping Tom, Mom," he said.

He waited and he waited. No closure. No neat little whirring act then disappearance into the night air. No resolution. Is it still in the apartment? Will it die and leave behind a hideous stench? Will I come upon its carcass when I clean behind the refrigerator in 2005? It's an unsolved mystery.

A thousand miles away I'd been unable to do a thing except commiserate with them and chuckle to myself. It makes my heart soar to know that, when faced with life's unpleasantries, my children can work things out together.

My Mother, The Bullfighter

It's not easy being the daughter of a bullfighter. I discovered that a long time ago. But then, as I grew, I realized my mother was only a bullfighter in her mind.

Years ago when my son, Jay, age 26, said, "Mom, your mother is a wild woman." I wasn't surprised. He finally had been one on one with her. She wasn't crazy about the idea of having *little* grandchildren. At 26 Jay was old enough, so she took him to lunch after he'd returned from a business trip.

She rarely asks about a person's daily life and doesn't have much use for talking about hers. But travel is special. She could talk endlessly about her trips. Mother hunted elk, moose, and bear. She killed one or two of each back when it was politically OK. She'd even had an article published in a major hunting magazine called, *I'll Go, But I Won't Shoot.* With help she caught huge fish in the waters off north Florida. Jay came home from lunch spellbound. This is not your usual Junior League woman.

But Mother isn't only a Wild Kingdom devotee. She and I share a love for opera, for all things Chopin, for eclairs, chocolate croissants, reading in bed, Nicholas, Alexandra, the little tsarinas, Rasputin, *I Love Lucy,* and pianists. We adored getting ourselves as brown as chocolate bunnies in the Caribbean and loved splashing in the sparkling 1950s waters off Jones Beach on Long Island. She was gleeful if anyone presented her with lobster or dark chocolate. She also downed frogs' legs whenever she could. Despite the legs, the lobster, and nasty-tasting dark chocolate, I adore her, even though her Russian soul sometimes flares up.

She climbed mountains and truly wanted to be a cowboy, one who could morph into a bullfighter. Wimpy cowgirl wouldn't do. Bullfighters were (perhaps still are) the highest specimen of mankind to her. Her best friend called her Toro. Somewhere she found and bought bullfighter's regalia, which she kept in her closet. I'm not sure if she ever wore it, but I tried on the hat from time to time.

"Be a bullfighter," she'd exhort me with her black eyes aflame, her spine stiffening. "You MUST do it," whatever it was. Jumping off a diving board, swimming in frigid water, going to camp when I begged not to go, learning to ride horseback ... I did them all. To challenge her was unthinkable. Mother told us often, curling her fists, "Mother is ALWAYS right."

Good grades in school were less important to her than being wild and crazy. Because of that, I spent most of my time writing stories instead of doing math and science. How she would have loved zany, daredevil daughters! Instead, she gave birth to three little girly girls, who weren't the boys my father wanted either — "Oh my God, Nanny, not another girl!" (Why *did* Dad call Mom Nanny?)

We were cowed in Mother's presence. She and Dad went off on trail rides, the wilder and more rugged the better. The accidents she had on the trail, such as when a horse bucked and threw her down a ravine, were her badge of honor.

We sisters cringed if she presented her rodeo-girl self to our friends, and were annoyed that they thought she was wonderful. They felt she was a refreshing change from their own pearl-proud, circle-pin-wearing mothers.

From my teen years I remember her best in faded blue jeans, but from deeper mines, I can see her in sensational ball gowns. ("Ball gowns! What a bourgeois sound that has," she would protest.) She managed to drag Dad to a dance once in a while. "Nanny," he'd plead with her, "I just did 300 pushups at the gym. Do we really have to go to the dance?"

"Puppy, je vous en prie," she would beg of him, knowing that beseeching Father in French would be irresistible. They both still did computations in French because of childhood lessons. He sat behind her in their classes in a little school in Switzerland and pulled her braids. "The Legend" says he dunked them in his inkwell.

"Please, Puppy? Viens!" Her small, compact body could insinuate a smile around his whole body. They stood in the kitchen arguing over what my father knew was written in stone. Of course she would win. Off to the ball they went while I was ecstatic to have peace in the house.

When she was in her fifties she'd sneak a glance at elderly people. "When I'm that old," she announced one day to her oldest daughter, Audrey, "just put me in a deluxe nursing home."

Audrey answered, to jolly things up, "Why *deluxe,* Mother?" Mother loved this comment, and repeated it to everyone.

As a child I'd watch Mother's Russian soul — she is of Armenian descent — switch in a flash from hot to cold, from loving to angry. Her charcoal eyes would deepen and her tongue would spit daggers at the closest target. Recently, I read that when people cannot deal with their own feelings, they come after yours. She and Father would have huge fits of anger, to the point where I would long for him to go off on one of his safaris. I wanted her all to myself.

Today, there is no sword of anger in her as she lies in her bed at her deluxe nursing home, her mind alternately switching on and off.

When I visit her, I accept her gradual still moments and wonder, *Where is she? Where is the feistiness?* I have so much to say, but we only talk in what she would have called "pedestrian conversation." She says little. "Who are these people?" she asked Audrey not long ago, pointing to pictures of her great-grandchildren. Audrey carefully pointed out who they were. Mother looked at her and said, "Well, how on earth would *you* know a thing like that and *I* would not?"

Recently, on her birthday, she asked Audrey eight times, "Who gave me this sweater?" Audrey told her eight times, and then said to her, "Mother, I've told you eight times!" Mother replied, "No, you haven't. Only seven." She was probably right. Mother is always right. The bullfighter lives.

A Cockroach
Is Not A Beautiful Thing

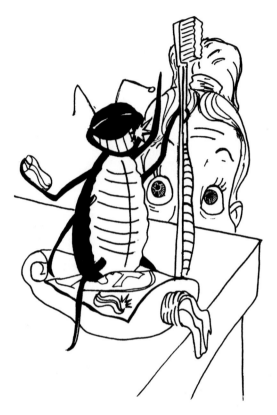

Six years ago, when we moved to Florida from Connecticut, I jumped at every piece of carpet fluff, certain it was a tropical invader of the crawling kind. My St. Vitus dance provided my husband hours of amusement. His blue eyes became slits as tears of laughter rolled down his cheeks.

The first time we had a visit from a "palmetto bug" was the day *after* the Buggy 'Bout Bugs Boys sprayed our house with who knows what. When the dog was still alive after an hour, we felt OK about breathing again.

May this house be safe from palmetto bugs, was my last thought as I drifted off to sleep that night in our Florida home. May they beat a path to somebody else's home, was my unneighborly thought.

The next morning, what to my innocent eyes should appear but a not-so-miniature you-know-what, furrowed brow and narrowed eyes. He … she?… was lolling comfortably on a jumbo tube of toothpaste. If you're thinking a roach was foraging in my medicine cabinet, I can assure you I haven't hidden a single Girl Scout cookie anywhere in a bathroom cabinet for decades.

As it turns out the critters like to eat toothpaste. "Yes, Ma'am," my new buddy said from the firm of Buggy 'Bout Bugs Boys. "Those critters have a powerful hankering for toothpaste." I got the message.

I can count on one hand the number of palmetto bugs we've seen in our home in the past six years: the time one appeared in the dog's chow, the time one was crawling among my diaries — *hello, those are private* — and the time my daughter visited. A groggy bug sidled up to her during cocktail hour. She didn't drop her six-month-old daughter. She clutched her darling tightly.

We used to call the bug guy to come and spray every time we had an encounter of the unpleasant kind. The cockroach contract said we could. Where there is one, *can an army be far behind?*

And then the unthinkable happened. We'd been lulled into not even thinking about roaches. None had surfaced in a year. But at 7:00 A.M., one fine day in the middle of October, as I pulled on a pair of jeans, I felt something moving around my calf. I pulled off my jeans, saw it clinging to my ankle, and flicked it off. My ankle, thumb, and forefinger had touched the monster. I was irrevocably sullied. Ruined.

"Sam," I yelled in my best fishmonger wife's yell, "get in here and deal with this!" I am woman. Hear me scream. Good thing I didn't say another thing: his eardrums would have been totally paralyzed.

He hunted the thing down and stomped on it — several times — until it made a huge splat on the front hall carpet, the one with scalloped shells. I made my usual female noises of how disgusting the whole thing was and how tremendous its girth was. "You could put a saddle on the damn thing, Sam."

And then something happened. I hate this, I decided. I don't need to let a cockroach win. I was tired of the ginger-ale-in-my-veins when a bug came within my range. What a bore to be such a wimp.

So, instead of getting down luggage from the crawl space and checking the Amtrak schedule to go north, where it only takes ten seconds, not a solid minute, to kill household pests, I decided to ... have a nice day. I browsed through books at the library, did the same at my favorite bookstore, investigated the new stores at Jacksonville Landing, and before I knew it, I'd had, indeed, a nice day.

An impromptu invasion is, no doubt, right around the corner. But for today, I am brave, though I know I could have a setback. The next intruding cockroach could be twice as big as the last one. It could bring a companion. It could even take a swat at me. But what about the phrase "Face your fear and do it anyway"? My goal is to be able to stomp on any uninvited creature myself. One stomp and done. I look through local college catalogs all the time for courses called "Killing Your North Florida Cockroaches." But no luck so far.

I should announce this one true thing: if I ever, *ever*, walk on one with my bare feet in the middle of the night, I'm outta here.

Bizarre Stuff
On The Road To Obscurity

"I WILL NOT TOLERATE ANY OF YOU BOYS LANDING ON THE FLOOR. PERIOD."

I am talking to three club sandwiches sliding around on the back seat of my Maxima, in danger of toppling to the floor. The sandwiches are, for the moment, in three neat Styrofoam boxes. I have just picked them up from Oak Bridge Club, less than a mile away. If the box lids pop open, and they fall to the floor, the mess from the bacon, turkey, tomatoes, side of fries, and cut-up fruit will be distressing.

I have a suspicion normal people don't refer to sandwiches as "you boys." I just spent my Saturday afternoon, one steamy July day, rewriting chapter six of my book. The last three months I've been in hibernation, scribbling on any forlorn piece of paper in my path, researching articles from *The New York Times* in the tub, dictating into a memo minder while walking, and fishing sales slips from my handbag to jot down notes to myself.

My husband tells me many nights while I lie sleeping my fingers tap dance on my pillow as though I am still working at my computer. Just as my dog races after cats in his sleep, I race after the truth, the truth I am seeking in a nonfiction book on volunteerism. At the moment the truth is that my sandwiches are about to behave badly.

When I walked into the club and stood at the bar waiting for my order to emerge from the kitchen, I felt I had walked into an episode of "The Twilight Zone." People were sitting around, chatting, drinking tasty beverages, watching tennis on a Titanic-sized TV. Others were outside playing golf, playing tennis, or dunking in the pool. People actually do this. I used to do it myself. Really. I remember the days fondly. I could do these things again and be good at the pool-dunking part. Especially good at the drinking-something-tasty part.

Members of Oak Bridge Club are charged a minimum fee and we're required to eat up because they'll bill us whether we eat or not. Any club that requires me to eat is OK with me. Today is a great day to have sandwiches for dinner, and my husband will love coming home from his volunteer job at B.E.A.K.S, the bird sanctuary, having cleaned huge bird cages since 7:30 A.M., hand fed the baby birds, and set wings on who knows how many pelicans and ospreys that have been bopped by golf balls. I feel smug. Dinner is ready and it's only 2:30.

Sandwiches are what I do best for dinners these days. And if my club sandwiches land on the floor, I'll be distraught. (But did I really call them "you boys"?)

It's exciting that I'm all set for dinner, but in addition, I have my lunch for tomorrow — the third sandwich. What a mastery of time saving. I should confess, though, that when "the boys" landed upside down on the floor the last time, when the Styrofoam lids popped open, it took a long time to mop up the mess. It threw my writing schedule way off.

When Sam arrived home at 6:30, he announced he had crashed, all six feet, one inch of him, on the grounds of the Sanctuary, tripping over a tree root. His teeth hurt, and his toenails, and all the good stuff in between. It was that kind of a fall. All he wanted for dinner was cottage cheese, he said.

Around midnight, as a treat for finalizing the seventh chapter of my book, I ate the second club sandwich. I don't know if I can face the third tomorrow. Those three sandwiches only cover part of what we have to eat up for the club minimum. I wonder if bartenders can sell take-out Margaritas and Bloody Marys.

***

I wrote about this for my writers' critique group, River City Writers. They seemed to like it, but then the critique took on a new dimension. JoAnn said, slowly, seriously, "Mims, why were the sandwiches ... 'boys?'" Claire offered, in her low, gentle voice, "Maybe if you make them corned beef it would sound more manly." Phyllis and I discussed the genders of egg, tuna, and chicken salad. The group broke off into factions. The feminist types lobbied for watercress, the ultimate female sandwich. Grilled Mahi-Mahi on a grinder? Definitely masculine. As they chatted, I zoned out. Can I throw together six peanut butter and jelly sandwiches when I get home? Oh the joy of it! Three whole nights of dinners in no time flat. It might be faster than driving to Oak Bridge and back. But wait: Sam only likes Smucker's Chunk-Style. You can't get that in Publix. I'll have to fly to New York, rent a car, drive to Finast, buy a jar, and race back to LaGuardia, in order to be home for dinner.

Writing is very complicated.

Sibby And I Get It Done

My middle sister Sibby and I reel with exhaustion after three sorry days, poking holes into decades of Mother's past. Sibby had flown to New York from Seattle to help dispose of Mom's three-bedroom apartment. Daddy died years ago. Now Mom is in a nursing home. The condo must be sold. I collapse a little weepy into my sister's arms saying, "Oh God. This sucks." (Did I really say that?)

We had been taking armloads of stuff downstairs to the dumpster. At one point she says, "I hate to think of strangers pawing their way through the garbage, looking at all of this." I look at the hundreds of loose snapshots of us — the three sisters, three graces, three harpies. Every third or fourth photograph seems to picture us as brides or debutantes. I tell her, raising one eyebrow, "Frankly, m'dear, they can paw all over our pictures if they want to!"

Sunlight is waning, the task, ending. Our backs ache from lugging Daddy's huge leather photograph albums. Twenty-three of them. The 1968-1969 album gets the creativity award for best juxtaposition: pictures of topless and big-busted African women from Dad's safaris sit near photos of us in low-cut ball gowns. *Oh Daddy, you're a scream. Did you plan that?*

Every photo is meticulously pasted in his albums. Christmases. Confirmations. Easters. "Do we have to stand still any more, Mummy? Make him stop." Graduations ... Vacations ... Weddings ... The stuff of the family of man, circa 1930s-1970s. Pictures of us fat, thin, cranky. Setting up the crèche, setting out in the newest Chevy convertible. Playing with teddy bears, playing the guitar. Gathered around Daddy's elephant tusks, gathered around the holiday turkey. We were gawky, we were glamorous, we were bored to smithereens, or giggly as jelly. Is it possible that we were once those little people? So innocent, unknowing about our futures? Are who and what and why we do things today spelled out among the recesses of these deep cupboards and cabinets?

We divide the silver, mineral collection, paperweights, and jewelry according to Mom's written wishes. I tuck all her musty clothes, reeking of mothballs, into black plastic bags, flexible plastic coffins going to Goodwill. Mother had a fixation about moths. You would have thought we had helicopters of moths dropping into the attic of our childhood home. Our clothes stank of mothballs for months after one of her mothball treatments.

It is 4:00 and we've been at this since 10:00 A.M. We're on a roll, my sister and I. "I'm told it's easier doing this while she's alive," Sibby assures me. We'll never know. The oddest piece of clothing is her fragile, ready-to-fall-apart honeymoon nightgown. "It's a Chanel from 1928," Mother told us countless times, pointing out the lacework at the throat. What an unsexy, shapeless, boxy affair for a 20-year-old bride. Perhaps it is a barely living prototype for "one size fits all." It was a strange choice made by this perpetually tiny, size eight woman.

Decisions about furniture, collectibles, clothing are easy — the hardware and software of our parents' lives. We brace ourselves to tackle the tough stuff in the den cabinet. Floor plans of the Larchmont house. The bronze die of our parents' wedding announcement. *Vogue* magazines from the 1920s. Six suede scrapbooks take center stage. They're bursting with glued-in memorabilia. It's a schoolgirl's summary of the early 20th century.

I have no stamina for this. So much stuff. So much. "Pitch it," I mutter, knowing I will be overruled. "They are her essence," my sister says with her gentle, big brown eyes, twins of mine. "They are her very being." How can I say no to that? So be it. We put them in a box for our third sister to pass judgment. She has not a scintilla of interest in any of this. Being the oldest, she is the liaison between Mother and us and the nursing home. A cheerless task.

On we go with this stop-and-go game of "Mother May I." We go full speed. Green light: pitch the frayed ribbons, bows, and used Christmas wrap. Yellow light: slow down for marriage certificates, huge sheets announcing Grandfather's graduation from a college in Istanbul, including a sheet of his academic record. Large scrolling numbers proclaim: History, eighty-nine; Geography, ninety-four.

Then, red light: full stop. It's our beloved uncle's senior yearbook from Collegiate School, complete with a short bio saying, Charlie "came from sad Armenia." We are stunned at this bizarre adjective. Sibby, more apt to be the saver, announces we can give a good Christian burial to a stack of his papers as he has no heirs. Amen.

I'm vaguely angry that my parents didn't weed out their stuff. Where do we draw the line with this? Keep the sketches of Mother's well-known artist friend? Toss all of Mother's and Dad's artistic piddlings?

Go ahead and grimace. Feel bad as you offer Dad's needlepoints and watercolors to the Goodwill box. Then, newspapers, which I keep: Lindbergh, the abdication of Edward, the walk on the moon, papers from Mother's day of birth and wedding day. We come upon an avalanche of slides. These we cannot face so we toss them wholesale holding our breath during this sacrilege, knowing we already have enough prints to cover a room the size of a garage --- ceiling, floor, and walls.

One box remains in the den cabinet. We are losing light and must hurry. My parents were selectively frugal: lamps are not abundant here. I dig into the box and ... "Look!" I say with glee. My sister stops her excavations and looks up. I tell her, "Money!" We both scream with laughter, tears rolling down our cheeks. It is a six-inch stack of worthless Russian money from the late 1890s, early 1900s. Why this strikes us funny we're not sure, but our tears are more from exhaustion than mirth. This treasure hunt never was about money, yet it would have been fun to find a cache of twenties tucked in a favorite navy handbag of hers.

I go home and wash my hands to scrub away the decades, trying to be rid of the stench of years of stale Arpege, laced with mildew and mold, and eau de mothballs. I flush away the grime of a century. But then I stop and think: do I really want to?

Free To Be
An Electronics Moron

A couple of weeks ago my husband, Sam, brought home a present for me. *He* called it a present. *I* called it a nightmare, a word he did not accept with grace. The so-called present was a "Freedom Phone." It didn't mean "cost free." But it did make me feel dumb. Perhaps "free to feel dumb."

After trying for two days to read the manual to (A) understand how to program the Caller I.D. and (B) learn how to punch in the code to dial one number instead of eleven, I decided to (C) quit. "I will return it," he said quietly. "No, don't return it, Sam," I said. "I *do* want it. Just read the manual and set it up for me." Simple. Then he said the thing that makes me regret that I learned to read: "You're a reader. Read the directions."

Nothing makes me sweat more than the words, "Read the directions." The reading directions controversy is where the entire man/woman, Mars/Venus thing comes in. We know about men and asking directions on the road. They don't. We do. Which brings me to computers.

Seventeen years ago, when Sam and I were newly married, my cut-and-paste editing with scissors amused but also exasperated him. He implored me to use a computer. But I liked writing first drafts on pink paper, second drafts on blue, third on yellow, and so on. Chivalry was not yet dead in our household, so he offered me an irresistible challenge: WordStar. "I'll show you a new function every day," he said. Patiently, he taught me WordStar, a software program now used by one person on this planet, maybe fewer. He knew WordStar perfectly, and we spent happy moments after supper — teacher and student — learning the finer points of WordStar.

***

I used it for a few years, then needed more up-to-date software. He suggested Word. I was all set to learn things from him, but he had never used it. "You're a big girl

121

now," he said. "You can teach yourself the program." Chivalry was now out the door, past the birdbath, and into our lake. I was frantic. I had deadlines and couldn't take half an hour to look up how you add French accent marks, or how you enter footnotes, or how to paginate.

"The damn page numbers ..."

"Get out the book."

I slammed down the manual and made a phone call. "Hello, Jean? Can you help me with Word?" Of course she said yes. Learning from other people (read "women") is how I learn best. To Sam, learning from a person, not a manual, is throwing in the towel.

I will admit I have bumbled onto some amazing discoveries by hitting a key accidentally. When I was asked to get invitations to a baby shower for my daughter's second child, I was fooling around on the keys and up popped baby bottles, festive cakes, balloons, and other printers' flotsam. So I designed the card myself, using a fancy border. It was incredibly tacky, but I was proud of it and even more proud of my daughter's response: she pretended it was cute. I've forgotten how on earth I can get those designs back. My daughter better not get pregnant again. (I'm happy to say she did, but nobody gives showers for a third pregnancy.)

Sam is, as I tell him often, "an incredible genius" when it comes to computers as well as other electronics, plumbing, wiring, and automotive repairs. I, myself, am happy that I can pump my own gas and punch in the numbers of the house's security code. I also know how to regulate my electric blanket in winter and use the broiler part of my toaster oven.

Sometimes, when Sam has been working for hours trying to repair a broken gadget in the house, he will announce, "I fixed it." The smile on his face is my cue. "Is this where I tell you you're an incredible genius?"

"Yes," he says. "It is."

***

This morning I noticed the beastly phone that I'd tried to program was sitting on a table in the far end of the living room. He hadn't returned it after all. Obviously he wanted it for himself in the first place. "I see you've kept the phone. Did you figure out how to do all the fancy things?" I asked.

"I don't need to use the bells and whistles," he said.

Does he mean it? Or has the incredible genius finally met his match?

Martha Stewart
Would Not Be Amused

It wasn't too long after my honeymoon that the realization hit me. I had to make dinner for my husband every night. A meat and potatoes deal. Except Sundays when I got away with soup and BLT's. How my friend Barbara seduced her husband into making dinner for twenty years I do not know. I supposed the operative word is seduce.

As for me, my copy of Peg Bracken's *I Hate to Cook Book* became dog-eared and stained. The pages often suffocated from the miasma arising from my stove. My handsome young ensign lovingly received my burnt offerings. "Stay-Abed Stew" was a particular favorite. You cooked it for five hours at 200 degrees — which causes food poisoning, doesn't it? Maybe not. We're still alive.

The best thing about my favorite cookbook was that most of the recipes were only six ingredients long. To this day, my eyes glaze over when I read about meals that require 12, 20 or more things to assemble. Six is the loveliest number. Fewer than six goodies and the meal feels a bit forlorn.

So when my friend June told me about a beloved family recipe from *Southern Living* called "Pineapple Cheese

Casserole," I had to try it. In five days, I would be having a board meeting/pot-luck supper at my house. Fifteen people. As hostess, all I had to do was set out iced tea and glasses and show up. But I wanted to contribute something special, although I felt the combination of pineapple and cheese was odd. I loathe the thought of pineapple pizza, or pineapple anything, but my favorite thing to cook is stuff I won't like, because then I won't be tempted to eat it.

When I need to drive to a new place, I often make a dry run. Attempting a new recipe for 15 people without doing a dry run did not sound like a good idea. I bought the ingredients: pineapple, cheddar cheese, sugar, butter, flour, and Ritz crackers. Six ingredients. The magic number. Because I'd been on a diet for one solid year, I hadn't eaten any of those things for one SOLID year. Not pineapple, not cheese, not sugar, butter, white flour, or crackers! Piece of cake, I said to myself, loving the irony. I'll make it and give it to Libby, my neighbor.

I thought it would be fun to assemble, and it was. As I grated the cheddar cheese, I smelled an aroma I hadn't smelled or tasted in ages. I'll have one bite, I said. One bite led to another, and before you could say, "Wake up and smell the soybeans," I realized I had eaten much of the pound of cheddar. But at least there was enough for the recipe.

Instead of chunks of pineapple, I had bought Dole's new cans of pineapple in "cosmic shapes": stars and moons. But as I mixed the fruit and cheese, all the pieces mushed up — they were far floppier than chunks. It looked more like pineapple sauce. The stars and moons had disappeared. No big deal.

I crushed the crackers in my right hand. It felt good to play with food. I hadn't done much cooking since my husband started living on cottage cheese and bagels. On my diet all I'd eaten was chicken, fish, eggs, a little beef, salad, berries, and an occasional potato.

I preheated the oven to 350 degrees, and then, absent-mindedly, set the casserole in the microwave (on top of the oven) and went into the living room to read the paper. Fifteen minutes later when I opened the *oven*, on the bottom, imagine my surprise to see that not only had the stars and moons disappeared, there was no dish in there at all! The concoction sat, room temperature, in the *microwave* looking pretty drippy. The crushed crackers and melted butter seemed tired. And to think that I was using my magic number of ingredients: six.

The potluck supper was a success without my contribution. The board members all brought plenty of yummy things to eat, and I made iced tea. That, I can do. And I remembered to show up.

Hot Pineapple Casserole

From June Lands

1   20 oz. can pineapple chunks

2   ½ cup sugar

3   3 Tbsp. flour

4   1 cup grated cheddar cheese

5   ¼ cup butter, melted

6   1/2 cup Ritz crackers, crushed

Preheat oven to 350 degrees. Drain pineapple. Reserve 3 Tbsp. juice. Combine sugar, flour, juice

Add cheese and pineapple. Mix well. Spoon into one quart greased casserole dish. Combine butter and cracker crumbs. Sprinkle over pineapple mix. Bake 30 minutes and serve.

I tried this again a few months ago, paid attention to the hard part (heating it) and it was scrumptious.

God, please be there.
This is a thank you note.

Dear God,

I'm not sure if I should be using a colon or a comma, but I have known you all my life and vice versa, so I guess the comma is okay. I would hope you'd use a comma with me. Feel free. On the other hand, I have written to a lot of CEOs and always used a colon, and if you aren't the chiefest of the chief executive officers, who is?

I'm thinking maybe I should send this to your branch manager, Mother Nature. I would send her a carbon copy, but she might consider it a slap in the face. And isn't "cc:" an antiquated idea? But then, maybe you're still using 1950s office equipment because it's perfectly good, cheaper than buying new, and who needs this all-new technology anyway?

Here's the reason for this letter: I want to thank you for thinking up menopause. I never thought of this phenomenon as "miraculous," but I do now. I realize what a good idea it is that women can't bear children throughout their entire adult lifetime.

For six weeks I helped my daughter with her brand new baby, Kallianne. (Thank you also for letting Melissa deliver two weeks early, but with her first baby, she was three weeks early, and boy, that was nice and, I'm really embarrassed about asking this, but do you think she could also be three weeks early for the next baby? That is, if you're good enough to let there be a next time, but really don't worry about it because they moved to Connecticut and prices are really high there, and I don't know if they can afford another child, and boy, I really have some nerve — it's the first letter I write you, and I'm into the fourth paragraph and nervy enough to ASK you for something, but God, God, I'm really nervous about sending this, because how do I know how fussy you are about punctuation and grammar and spelling?)

And how do I send this anyway? Airmail? Special Delivery? Certified Mail, Return Receipt Requested? Special Priority?

Anyway, God, I've just begun to understand the phrase "Life begins at 50." When I raised children, it never occurred to me that caring for children day in, day out was a sacrifice, but now I understand. Take my life now. (Oh God, God, that was not a request! I better watch my language.) I'll rephrase. Consider my life now. My date book includes lunch with Eileen, Monday; Debbie and Eva, Tuesday; Bill and Bunny, Wednesday; lunch with the gang at Borders on Thursday; and then dinner with Sam, Friday. This is not work. Children are. And while I adore my grandchildren from here to ... well, your neck of the woods, I am so happy you didn't make it possible for us to bear babies our whole life long.

When I helped my daughter after her second child was born, here was the schedule: at 9:00 A.M., my daughter went out for groceries. I'd hold the baby the whole time because her mornings are fussy. I'd watch two-year-old Mackenzie take clean clothes out of her drawers and put them in the laundry machine, or watch her do a load of crayons in the dishwasher while I changed the baby. I'd race after her as she'd dip a bubble blower in the toilet or blow bubbles over the glass coffee table. When Melissa came back from Publix we'd both vacuum and dust, and tidy up because realtors were coming to show the house.

So, now it's noonish and time to feed the older baby, do laundry, load the dishwasher, and take the children to the park to let the fresh air wear them out. On our way home we'd stop at the dry cleaners and finally a trip to Publix, so Mackenzie can race straight up the aisle to the balloons (pronounced "beeyoons.")

When we all came home, because I am 55, as I regularly remind my daughter, I had an excuse to nap. My daughter asked me once, after the first baby was born, "Are you worn out?"

"Of course not," I snapped. She said, "Me neither." When I grew up, if people in our family admitted to being tired they were considered weak. This reminds me of another topic I'd like to bring up: Is it a sin to take a nap? I seem to be one of the rare ones in the family who loves to nap.

Did I get a "Loves to Nap" gene? Take my Aunt Alice. (Don't really *take* her, Lord, just *consider* her.) Napping is unthinkable to Alice. But then she did have monkey gland injections when she was middle aged, for energy.

"Tsk, tsk," 100-year-old Alice says to her sister, my nonagenarian mother. "Napping? What do you mean Babsy's napping?" Alice rocks her whole body in a visible staccato. She is in high dudgeon. We constantly ask Alice not to call and wake Mother every day at 3:00. Mother naps at that time but is too embarrassed to admit it. Alice, again: "Nap? What is there to nap about? She's on her bed all day long! I will call her at 3:00. That's my best time to call." My aunt has a busy schedule. From her room in the hospital's elderly nursing care wing, she is a volunteer stapler. She staples for the development office. She may possibly be the "Oldest Living Stapler."

Anyway, I've been wanting to ask you: Did you forget to give Aunt Alice the slowing-down mechanism that comes with menopause? We're all grateful that she staples, because God knows what mischief she'd get into otherwise. (Maybe you can tell us.) Is she the one person on earth who hasn't gone through menopause? Or was it the monkey glands? I don't think Alice ever went through menopause. She never had any children. Maybe that's why she's still stapling at age 100.

I have no shame about napping. I figure anyone who has gone through menopause deserves two things: no more children and plenty of naps. Anyway, thank you for giving us a way of getting out of becoming pregnant.

And God, don't feel bad when women moan about menopause. It was a great idea. One last thing: I just realized I haven't the vaguest idea how much postage to put on this, so could you please sign up for e-mail?

Insanity On A Crystal Clear Day

In the past ten years since moving to the Jacksonville area I've met dozens of people who love to write. Amazing, talented writers. I've met them in writing classes, ones I've given and taken, and I've met them at writers' conferences. When I see them I remember their memoirs. I run into writers in Stein Mart, at the beach, and at church, and I think about their funny stories as they grew up in the South or their tales about surviving the Depression. Writers' roundtables abound. There's my own writers' group that supports and encourages week after week. So many people nowadays are writing their life histories for their children and grandchildren.

I've been thinking about writers a lot these days and hoping they are writing down the insanity of what happened one crystal clear autumn day in 2001, in what we blithely called, "a New York minute." Are they recording their feelings about the weeks and months after 9/11 for their children and grandchildren? People are surely saving magazines and newspapers about the attack. But are they writing about their *personal* remembrances for future generations?

How I would love to read from my mother's or grandmother's diary, to discover how they felt during the days surrounding Pearl Harbor. My children used to ask, "What was it like when JFK died?" My granddaughters are nine months, three years, and five years old. What will I tell them when they're old enough to ask, "What was it like?" Recording even a crazy quilt of memories and feelings is a gift. Writing it is a salve for the soul, as all memoir writing is.

Random snippets from my diary, September 11, 2001 ... At 3:00 P.M. I watch events unfold, once again, as I sit in the dentist's chair, watching his overhead TV. I have watched the attacks on the World Trade Center over and over all day. I am having a root canal. I feel the five sticks of novocaine. Wincing, I recoil with disgust that I let them bother me.

The phones are out in New York, but my sister (who lives on 84th Street in Manhattan) e-mailed, "It is eerily silent out there. I am looking down on people trudging past my window. I look downtown and see smoke; I look uptown and there is nothing."

September 12 ... The sadness in the pit of my stomach is ongoing. A three-day nor'easter makes it impossible to walk Charliedog, so I am penned in, watching TV all day, all night, seeing the slo-mo collapse of the city where I was born.

Melissa (my daughter) tells me horror stories of people in her town, Darien, Connecticut. Young mothers have husbands missing, friends have lost friends, and some have no more jobs because their offices have been shattered into a million pieces. There are miracle stories about husbands who didn't go to their jobs at the World Trade Center because of doctors' appointments near home or meetings with clients in Greenwich.

September 13 ... It's getting worse. I am still numb. The first two days you're strong, but the repeated scenes on TV and the doleful music makes the soul ache. Taglines on TV uniformly title the event "Attack on America." I cannot stop watching TV. I asked Melissa what she's telling her tiny children about the attack. She says she tries not to have the TV on, but told the four year old it was "an accident."

September 14 ... We went to a musical show last night, *Pump Boys and Dinettes*. We had a hard time mobilizing ourselves for an evening out with friends. But the rollicking music took reality away for two hours. At the end the cast collected money for the Red Cross. We had a Candlelight Vigil and sang "God Bless America" outdoors.

September 15 ... A normally devil-may-care New York friend describes NYC and herself as being terrified ... *that* scares me. I waited in line two hours to pay for an American flag. Flags are everywhere. I cannot believe our country is preparing for war.

September 16 ... Now the taglines proclaim, "America Rising." Radio is telling people NOT to listen to radio! They're telling us to take a break from the news. I heard a mother say that her child, being told his father was dead, said, "Can I call him on the cell phone?" Another child, being told God was pulling people up to Heaven said, "Does he have enough hands?"

September 17 ... When I walk in the morning, I say, "Morning." Today I felt I was saying, "Mourning." Maybe tomorrow it will be, "Good Mourning." I wish I could get from sad to angry. Angry is better. I cleaned up endless debris from the storm and was amused at the words "clean-up," when I think about the clean-up in New York.

September 18 ... It's so good to see commercials back on TV. A glimmer of normalcy ... I wore my old New York

136

City sweatshirt today with the billowing trees of Central Park imprinted on it. I looked down at the shirt and realized the World Trade Center was imprinted in the background.

September 19 ... Today, I laughed a bit for the first time and it felt so good. Melissa wanted to run out and get the mail so she asked little Mackenzie to hold her baby sister, only a few months old. Mackenzie spied the ice cream truck outside, and, after carefully cradling the newborn between blankets on the floor, she ran outside to get a cone. Priorities! An 8th grader at a local school is collecting new teddy bears to send to saddened NYC children. I bought five at Target and took them to the school. It made me feel better. But then this: Mackenzie found out her brand-new best friend Crosbie, a preschooler, couldn't play because she was going on a trip. Mackenzie sat, pensive, and then said, "I hope she doesn't have to fly, Mama."

Goo, Glorious Goo

I would not call myself a chronic abuser of QVC. Fifteen years ago I ordered a pasta maker from that channel. It came with a video — a novelty in the mid-eighties. I studied it and within a day was making spaghetti to die for. Die really quickly, choking on the lumps of dough. We quickly got tired of lumpy spaghetti, even though I bought the lumpiest tomato sauce in hopes of disguising the problem. I gave up. Ronzoni never tasted better. As for the fate of the machine, my stepdaughter warehouses it on her top kitchen shelf.

Which brings me to my paraffin bath. Two weeks ago, in a fit of boredom, on a cold and rainy Monday, I channel-surfed my way to QVC. A Remington Paraffin Spa from the Spa Therapy Collection, featuring Aromatherapy Wax, was on the screen. It promised to "ease stiff joints and sore, tired muscles." I was thinking of using it on my feet. The TV ladies said, "The bath accommodates up to a woman's size 10 shoe." So far so good. Vibrating hand mitts came with the bath. I could "winterize" my rough hands too.

For ten minutes I was mesmerized listening to viewers' testimonials. My hand inched toward my MasterCard. You buy, you fly, girl. Here it was, 10:00 A.M. Monday, and I hadn't bought a single thing all day. The economy was suffering without me. Buying my spa over the phone took 30 seconds and cost something around $60. For $20 more I ordered a huge amount of extra wax. Sixteen pounds. I didn't realize the wax could be used over and over. My supply will outlive me. I had planned to be cremated but, in the interest of thrift, perhaps a volunteer can warm the wax, pour the leftover stuff on me and keep me company while I disintegrate. ("I'm melting!" Think *Wizard of Oz*.) Actually, it should be toasty sensation. I chose a lemon scent.

A gigantic box arrived within days. I ooh'd and ahh'd. What a pleasure! A paraffin bath in my home. No video, just a 12-page book of instructions. I didn't need to go to a salon and pay money each time for a paraffin bath. (On the other hand, I never HAD gone out and gotten a paraffin treatment at a store.)

The wax arrived hard, solid. I dumped in the required amount — four pounds — and, at 7:30 P.M., turned the machine on HIGH. It would take 1 1/2 hours to melt.

I checked on the wax periodically and watched it become a glorious taffy-goo. At 9:00 P.M. sharp, I did exactly what the ladies on TV did — I immersed my right hand up to my wrist into the length of the pool of lemony liquid wax. The pain was so intense I screamed. (Think final stages of labor.) The ladies had dunked their hands five times. So did I. After the second immersion I turned the heat to LOW. The temperature was not LOW soon enough. I danced around the bathroom for a minute, in hopes of cooling the wax, then rolled it off to see how my hand was doing. It was doing great! Soft and silky.

Next the feet. They were more complicated. After I dunked them, I hit a snag. I sat on the bathtub rim, trying not to topple into the tub. I had a hard time pulling off the wax. It didn't come off in long "pulls" like taffy. I had to flick little pieces off my fingers and some of it landed on my green carpeting. Charlie, "The Dog Who Eats Anything," downed gobs of wax despite my hollering at him. I couldn't chase after him or I'd get footprints of wax on my wall-to-wall bathroom carpet.

What I learned from my spa experience is this: if you want to get your dog to poop less often, get a paraffin spa. Wax is constipating. Perhaps my stepdaughter has some more room on her shelves.

Star Struck In 32082

I was walking along — in my usual way, on my usual path, at my usual time — when whom did I see but Annette Bening. She smiled a broad grin and ran past, all athletic looking. She waved cheerily and I waved back as though we'd known each other for years. I was so thrilled I almost turned around and followed her, but I'm glad I didn't because who was rounding the curve to Lakeside? Robert DeNiro. He was absorbed in his pace walking, and his face told me the "Hi" would go unreturned, so I left him alone. It was seeing Ernest Hemingway that made me realize I was having a bizarre day, and that I needed to go home and take a nap. But, honestly, I have had a few brushes with stars.

Many years ago at a Broadway theater, when I slid to my seat along a row of theater-goers who courteously stood up for me, I looked at the face of my theater partner, and recognized the now-deceased Carroll O'Connor. "Oh, my God. It's YOU," I said. He smiled weakly, bowed, and sat down. In an instant I realized I wouldn't be able to concentrate for one minute on *The Beauty Queen of Leenane* with him right next to me. More importantly I wanted *him* to know I wouldn't bother him like a dithering fan. "So," I said to him as the house lights faded, "I'm not going to say a word to you." I moved to an empty seat, one away from the actor.

For the whole first act it worried me that the dear man whom I admired greatly took that to mean I didn't like him. That I didn't approve of his work. That I didn't like *All in the Family*. (I loved it.) The lights faded and the drama started. Whole hunks of dialog flew by as I tried to fashion what I'd say to him during intermission. I got out my penlight and made notes on my *Playbill*. At intermission a line of admirers in the row in front of us turned around and we all chatted.

When we lived in Los Angeles, my husband and I were on a mini-vacation in a Westwood hotel and guess who walked onto the elevator with me? Dustin Hoffman. He was dressed only in a towel around his waist, probably on his way to a massage. He had one of his semi-smirks on his face. I couldn't think of a thing to say. Maybe that was a good thing.

But most exciting is that I lived for years right next to Jeffrey DeMunn in Stamford, Connecticut, until he moved. He was the star of Arthur Miller's *The Price* on Broadway and nominated for a Tony. His movie *The Green Mile* won an Academy nomination for best picture, and he's been in many Stephen King TV mini-series, plus *The X-Files* and dozens of movies. One morning, about 10:30, I'd just flown up from Florida. I was hoping to see his lady friend so I could tell her to relate to Jeff how excited I was about his success in the play. I threw my suitcase in my apartment, and rang Jeff's door. When Jeff himself opened the door, looking disheveled, I was stunned. I clasped my hands and carried on about how excited my whole family was for him.

Then I realized it was Saturday morning. The man had two performances that day. He was probably trying to sleep late. I took in a huge gulp of air and said, "OMIGOD, Jeff! You were probably sleeping! I'm so sorry." Graciously he said, "That's OK. I've already had coffee."

Good thing there aren't a lot of celebrities in this town for me to harass.

Anonymity Is A Good Thing

Faith Ford, who was on *The Murphy Brown Show*, was excited about her new spin-off TV show, but she loathed the New York City buses displaying gigantic pictures of her face. "Oh God, " she said. "I just die when I see those buses." I, personally, am giddy with relief that my face is not on a bus.

When I was in third grade, I was two "me's." One me went to school and was a model child. "I hate being a model child," I remember complaining to my mother, when she told a friend how perfect I was. There was nothing I could do about it.

When Mom left the house, I turned into a whole different me. I'd listen to the tires crunch up the driveway and onto the lane. Then I'd turn up my record player and, like a million other third graders with Broadway aspirations, belt out "The Lady is a Tramp," "I Could Have Danced All Night," or "Let Me Entertain You." I'd be Peggy Lee or Doris Day. My eight-year old actress name was Holly Chapelle.

And then, eight years later — calamity. I tried out for the role of Amahl in the operetta *Amahl and the Night Visitors*. It was the Christmas play inexplicably chosen by the music teacher, Miss Overwein, for the junior and senior classes, which averaged 20 girls to a class. I didn't get the role of Amahl. I didn't get the role of a lamb or a sheep, either. I was merely Melchoir's *understudy*. *Oh the ignominy!* I closed a chapter of my life and jumped with both feet — hands, really — into writing. I began to type. From Broadway Star to Bard in a single leap. No crutches.

Forty years later, and 100 rejections for every 10 articles published, I am finally at peace. What a relief that producers are not squatting on my doorstep, begging me to schmooze on late-night, lite TV. Publishers aren't crawling up A1A, sobbing because I've turned down the screen rights to my bestsellers. If you could see me now, you'd see me in a hammock with my tall beverage pole, stuck in the grass, offering me an iced raspberry tea. Florida living's taught me time out is delicious. I don't sing, "Fame! I'm gonna live forever!" I sing out with Celine, top of my lungs, as I tootle along in my convertible. And I don't have to worry about my lack of lipstick if somebody is idling next to me at a red light.

I'm a poster woman for Intensely Private Person. I don't much like it when my name is called out at Zimmiz Hair Designers. I cringe when the nurse with the loudest voice bellows it in full earshot of 60 other patients when I go for a blood test.

I cannot imagine going to dinner with my husband, Sam, and having to look animated and charming because a photographer is angling to *take a shot of me!*

And furthermore, if I were famous, I'd have to think about Sam's clothing.

"Are we going out to dinner?" Sam asks every Friday night, week in, week out. Sometimes I just want to zip over to eat at Lulu's, a half mile away. Nevertheless, I rally: "Wheredoyouwanttogo?"

"I dunno. You pick it." He is dressed to the nines in his "Nuke the Gay Whales For Jesus" tee shirt. I debate whether he's going to change into a guayabera shirt — his Aruban taxi driver's shirt. I suggest Mexican food. He'll say we'll never be able to park. Here he goes:

"Are you kidding? You know we can never find a place to park."

Bingo. "How about ..." I choose three other restaurants. I'm bored already and we still haven't turned the key in the ignition.

I read somewhere that the Duke and Duchess of Windsor recited the alphabet to each other when they were bored in restaurants and ran out of things to talk about. Perhaps the Duchess was so skinny from the angst she felt when dining out. Maybe they felt the public would think they were fighting if they didn't talk to one another. For me being an unknown means I can eat more rolls than I should. I can pick at Sam's dessert. Turn my glass of water into a lemon drink by asking for lemons, and not have to pay for lemonade. So help me, if people asked me for an autograph while I was eating, I'd smile and make them stand there till I was finished.

And how about fans who follow stars into the bathroom? Kathie Lee Gifford said someone once passed her a piece of paper from under the stall next to hers and said, "Honey, could you sign this for my niece, Charlene?"

"Honey," I would inform the interloper, "I am in here on serious business. Sorr-ee, no." And the next day *The Star* would write a feature story about how a woman in a public restroom and I got into a huge brawl. She'd be quoted saying I sent her whole body crashing into the hand dryer because I wouldn't give her an autograph for

Charlene, dying of multiple myeloma, chlamydia, and the heartbreak of psoriasis.

I value my privacy too much to love fame. The other day I hid my writing from the folks who clean our house. *This is pretty ridiculous. Some of the work I'm hiding is given out free in restaurants.* I guess I've learned to believe what columnist Liz Smith says about stars: "Stars don't behave, think, hire, or fire like ordinary people."

I've learned to love ordinary. Given myself permission to be ordinary. Ordinary is a beautiful thing. As Anne LaMott says in *Traveling Mercies*, "Sometimes … you need to hang out in ordinariness." On my tombstone it should say no name. Just "Anonymous." And underneath that, "She was ordinary and just fine about it."

Of course…on the other hand…I could change my mind about all of this…

The Day The Roof Didn't Fall

I never thought I could fall in love with my roofer, but I did the day L.C. entered my life. A few weeks ago, when I got an estimate on a total re-roofing, I grumbled. It would take two weeks to complete and cost two-thirds the price of a zingy foreign car. Add the noise, the inconvenience, the mess ... well, who needs it?

I needed it. "Real bad," as the roofing contractor said. He said the old roof was a mess. That's all the information you're going to get about the roof's condition because I blank out when men talk about roofs, electricity, and pressure washing.

Well, I bit the bullet, signed a contract, and two weeks ago, ten eighteen-year-old boys were climbing like monkeys all over my incredibly steep roof. I wanted to holler, "Do your mothers know you're doing this?" I wanted to tell them they needed better shoes if they were going to tramp around on peoples' roofs. But I told myself to get a grip. They were NOT kids. They had probably been doing this all their lives, albeit short ones. Looking up at them, scrambling up there, a bazillion feet in the air, I said to one guy, still on the ground, "Boy, I'd sure be scared doing that," and to my disbelief he said, "Yes, ma'am. Some of us are."

But to get to L.C., the foreman and CEO of this job. L.C. is a hunk, really buff, and incredibly tanned, great smile. I know he's buff because he works with no shirt on — not even a tee shirt. The second week the weather turned cold and he put his clothes back on. Bummer. I liked ogling his ripply muscles.

Beyond the tan and the sexy body, here's what makes this 58-year-old woman's heart go pitty-pat over a guy who is probably no more than 27. (Is this a good place to say that I have a 33-year-old son?)

I picked L.C. over the other nine contenders (contenders — I'm not sure for what) for his eyes, his cute face, and most of all, his adorable southern accent. As a former northerner of 45 years, I find it hilarious when a man of any age says to me, "Yes, ma'am." Nobody up north ever called me "ma'am." Every opportunity I had, I'd ask L.C. what I hoped would be a bright question.

Talking with someone on your steep, angled roof can be dangerous. So when I noticed L.C. was climbing down, I'd leap out of my chair, go outside, hoping to talk to L.C. while I walked the dog. I didn't want to seem forward. Charliedog loves having roofers. Today one of the guys said to me, all polite, "You do walk that dog a lot!"

One day toward the end of the job, when L.C. was working on the roof over my bedroom, I fantasized that the ceiling caved in, right over my bed. And he fell right next to me, on my bedspread. I needed to lie down on the bed a lot that day. I told myself I was light-headed and should remain prone like Cleopatra on her barge. She was said to be comfortable in the presence of powerful men. I now know why she was on that barge so much.

Bangbangbangbangbangbang. The noisy machinery that insistently banged on the shingles in rhythmical sequence continued. *You're not chained to this part of the house,* I told myself. But then I won't be here when the roof collapses and L.C. falls down next to me, props himself up on his elbows and says, "Hey! How are ya doin'?" I suppose I could have thought of sexier things that he might have said, but I'm out of practice.

The roof's almost finished. Today is the guys' last day. I probably won't need a new roof for 40 years. L.C. will be 67; I will be 98.

My bones began to ache from lying on the bed so long. Reluctantly, I got up off my bed and baked chocolate chip cookies for all the roofers. You know the old saying, "The way to a roofer's heart is through his stomach." Ah, me. Ah, sweet fantasy of life.

Charliedog's going to miss his six walks a day.

Launching A Wedding

I've never been much for giving parties. You would think, having birthed a female child, that I'd be ready to launch her wedding. I had 23 years to plan, and as Melissa and Dave had dated each other for seven years, I should have known Dave would eventually ask her to marry him.

When they visited Florida one April, I didn't suspect a thing. Dave asked me if there was a nice place in Jacksonville to go on a picnic. I suggested Hanna Park. When they returned he said, "That place was great. I asked your daughter to marry me!"

As goose bumps settled in, I hugged them both, then rummaged in my files and was surprised to see I'd gathered two fat folders full of stuff about weddings and receptions — stuff I'd been saving for three years. I was hoping Dave would be her choice. I plopped my bulging "Wedding" files into Dave's arms, hugged him and said, "Here you are! You guys want to have fun planning it?"

"Oh Mom," my daughter groaned. My husband has always called me "Mims the Organizer." They wanted a traditional wedding, meaning a traditional mother doing the arrangements.

Let the phone calls to relatives begin. My 95-year-old aunt's reaction was the most blasé. "I'm getting married, Aunt Alice," my daughter said. "Hmmm," said Alice, moving right along. "How's the water temperature down there?" Melissa covered the phone and told me with disbelief what Alice said. Did Alice mean the temperature at the ocean or in our house faucets? When Melissa told her the wedding date, Alice said, "NOT FOR A WHOLE YEAR?" But then Alice was not buying green bananas at her advanced age. (She eventually died at the age of 101, in 2000, having lived in three centuries.)

I had hoped the couple would elope but should have known better. And now, here we were, 11 months to countdown. I bought one of those hefty magazines for brides, one so large it rivals my husband's *Computer Warehouse* catalogs. I settled in with this magazine of a thousand gowns and suddenly I was a mother-in-law to be.

In bed one night, I flipped through *Brides Today* while Sam was drifting off to sleep. We were planning on spending a reasonable amount on the dress, but I needed to scare him with ridiculous prices so the dress we would pick would appear to be a bargain. "Look Sam," I said, "Can you believe it? This dress costs $3,000." He groaned. A few minutes later I tugged the sheets to wake him up. "Honey? Look at this. Can you imagine? It's $6,000."

"Can't you get her something at Pic 'N Save?" he said. Luckily for Melissa the local store went out of business.

Songadeewin Camp,
Of Thee I Sing

It's 8:00 P.M., Gate 15A, Miami International Airport. It's been pouring for an hour and the tarmac is slick with rain. Three women seated near me, strangers, interrupt my concentration as I hunch over a crossword puzzle. They are playing "One-upmanship," the travel version. It's a game I cannot understand. They buzz about Paris, cluck over Barcelona, thrill to thoughts of Vienna. And once they've saturated themselves and oozed long enough over love talk about Europe, they start in on America. Baltimore, Chicago, San Francisco. It's name dropping, city style.

I've been away from home for a long five days. My maximum comfort zone — the longest I can happily be away — is three days. OK maybe a week. I am so eager to be headed home that I left for the airport four hours too soon. I feel deliciously free, sitting with a rich supply of ink around me: *USA Today*, *The New York Times*, and *The Wall Street Journal*. If the airport knew the delight this ardent news junkie takes in the smell of the newsprint, they would charge me an admission fee.

Home. What a beautiful word. I am childlike in my yearning to pull into my driveway. My romance with "home" goes back a long way.

***

It is hot and steamy on this June day in 1954. I am eleven. Mother takes me by the hand from our New York apartment to a cab and on to Grand Central Station. I'm pleading not to go. The overnight train trip with dozens of other eleven-year-old campers frightens me. I know none of them. For a fearful city child, going off to camp holds no promise of adventure in the White Mountains of Vermont.

I perceive the eight weeks at Songadeewin of Keewaydin Camp for exactly what they are: two months of my parents' not having to think up what to do with me during school vacation. In the 1950s, children did not fight to win. We fought a little for things we wanted, but not the way children do today, not to the finish.

It has taken me decades to realize why I am so attached to home base. It dawned on me while I listened to the women at this Airport verbally prance all over the world: I was raised in a family of travelers, and instead of being allowed to go with them, was made to go to camp for almost all summer. When I became an adult and could choose to travel, I balked. *I can be home now. I'm old enough to ... stay at home.*

I am so excited to have figured out why I hate to travel that I make a long distance cell call to my sister in Seattle. "That's child abuse," she says. "I had no idea you hated camp. Mother used to tell me 'Miggy loves her Songa.'" When we hang up I want to embrace her. I am justified. She doesn't poo poo me. She listens, she sympathizes. We are angry with Mother, a rarity. I had to travel (go to camp), and now I can decide for myself if I want to travel. And I choose not to.

Home from my trip the next day, with the mail read, the papers skimmed, and the laundry on "Spin," I take out my diaries from 1954-1957, when I was 11 to14 years old, the years that cover my four years at Songa. I want to verify the loathing I still feel for it and the injustice done to me. The first year's journal says, in perfect fourth grade penmanship: "Tuesday, June 28, 1954: Leave for camp! Slight case of homesickness. Sleep on the train. Hung around with Brenda. Maw and Sib come to the train." The next day: "Miserable case of homesickness on bus. I love the place now that I'm here. Get two bunk mates Carolyn Buckley and Josephine Murphy." And the next: "It's raining so we play cards. Have our medicals then swimming. Go riding and have archery. I love archery and I'm reather (sic) good."

The next two days are blank. Then, this: "I love Songadeewin. Nearly made a bull's-eye in archery. Had glee club and dancing and games. Hate dancing." The next week the diary tells me that I am on the White Team. I am a fanatic White. Mr. Harter (camp owner) in a "solem proceedger" gives us our cinnabas — "a long strip of something that feels like a shammy."

We all wear these around our neck and covet these "cinnabas" (no such word in Webster's Unabridged) more than any medal of honor. Each week we are given a rubber stamp announcing our accomplishments in various sports. In my shameless competitiveness, I am dying to have my cinnaba stamped all the way around it with my accomplishments.

Week after week, every Tuesday, I dutifully record my stamps: July 26: "Have council fire. Get stamps in archery tennis and drama." July 28: "Today is Songadeewin Sunday. Inishiation Day. Girls who have been here four years have to do crazy mixed up things." I crave to be a four-year camper. By August 8 I have 50 points on my cinnaba, including one stamp for canoeing, because I was in the "Canoe Meat." I got to ride Vicky, my favorite horse, and my day was made.

I slog on, reading through four years at camp, four years of highs and lows, fighting with bunk mates, doing things that get me and my buddies in trouble. I reminisce about putting our bunks out on the porch, trips to St. Johnsbury for sugaring off, 10-mile hikes, overnights in sleeping bags (practically on top of cow pies), days of more "canoe meets," eventually spelled correctly, as is "initiation." Despite the fact that the Greens won the cup more years than we Whites liked, I write, in late August of 1957: "I sob uncontrollably" on the last day of camp.

How do you like that? I did like camp after all. Another theory shot down. Sometimes you need to read an old diary to set the record straight.

Good Old Glory

Going to overnight camp, on Lake Willoughby, in Barton, Vermont, for four years, eight weeks each year, you become pretty familiar with the American flag. We watched it being raised smartly in the morning, and we watched it being put to bed. The best thing about reveille? Breakfast was right around the corner. Breakfast was red, white, and blue, too. Big Vermont-grown blueberries, seas of white milk from Vermont cows, and the reddest of red raspberries, New England's finest, perfect for making smiley faces on our pancakes.

Cut to four decades later. Like so many of us, I never got around to putting up an American flag. On September

17th, 2001, I found out where I could get my American flag. I drove up Beach Boulevard into Jacksonville. Driving into the sizable parking lot, I found cars parked every which way. They were on an adjacent side street, parked sloppily on peoples' lawns, spilling halfway into driveways. Careless drivers had gouged out deep ruts, making holes that threatened to swallow the cars whole. Inside the store, it was a madhouse. People waiting to pay snaked in a line around the store for two hours. I was one of the lucky ones. I did get a flag, a beauty, three feet by five, hand stitched, not printed. It was 2:00 P.M. when I got there. By 3:00 the store was sold out. I didn't know it would take me two weeks to find a pole and holder.

Finally, it was up. A couple of nails on my house, and voila! A flag. THE flag. MY flag. I made a vow not to be like some people who leave their flag out all night long and when it rains.

The first time I put it up it was already 4:00 o' clock so it could only be up for a short time before I had to take it down, at dusk. I cradled it in my arms. I folded it 'round and 'round its pole, brought it inside, and laid it, well this sounds irreverent, but I laid it on top of the dog's cage. It was the nearest thing to the front door. I quickly discovered that if I stood the pole by the door, the whole flag drooped onto the floor. And though my dining room table probably would have made a better mattress for my

161

flag, I am not so patriotic that I want to risk wrecking my wood finish. I thought about wrapping a rubber band around it, but I didn't want it to feel any pain.

In the morning I awoke thinking, "Oh goody, I can put up my flag." And as I did, an amazing thing happened: A rousing melody I haven't heard in four decades played in my head. It was a bugle call, ringing out as loud as if it were blaring from a window on the second floor. It made me giggle because it sounded like a pretty good accompaniment to a "flag raising."

The same melody played inside my brain every morning for a week or so, until finally I wondered if it could be the song I heard so long ago, on the banks of Lake Willoughby. My husband did a little fiddling on the Internet and came up with a website that plays the more than a dozen songs performed by the armed services from reveille to taps. I listened to the first one...then the next. "Did you find the one you've been hearing in your head?" he asked.

Sure enough, I did.

My Strawberry Basket

"Fat burns in the presence of oxygen," Jane Fonda says on one of her aerobics walking tapes. I breathe in and out as hard as I can, envisioning a huge straw basket, the kind used to pick strawberries on a hot summer day in Vermont. I try to fill up the basket with my breath.

Today's listening tape is not Jane Fonda's. It's Mr. Sousa's rousing parade music, perfect for walking and far more energizing than Rush Limbaugh, NPR, or any book-on-tape.

I trot along, walking beside Charlie, my eight-pound mini poodle, who bounces in rhythm with his own band. He's searching for a treat at this early hour. A squashed frog will do just fine. Or a succulent, semi-comatose worm, with a trace of a wiggle. "When he barfs it up," Sam told me one time, "we can call him Chuck. Short for Upchuck, of course." Bon appetit, Charlie. Sorry I can't join you.

I lop off a lime from the neighbors' tree — with their permission — and pass through the bike path onto the main road. Soon I nod to the usual gang. An older couple in their 80's holds hands as they always do. She clasps a Publix bag and picks up trash along the way every day. Farther on there's a courtly gentleman with a mustache and Charlie Chaplin legs who always says "Good day." There's a triumvirate of biker-moms. And that woman with the world's sourest look on her face. I want to shake her and tell her to smile, for God's sake. It's a beautiful world out there. And of course there's the woman training for a triathlon to whom I want to bow down.

And then ... there they are. I noticed them a year ago. I saw him alone at first and tried to get him to nod. But he never did until one day he was running with a lovely girl by his side. That day, he said hello to me. Clearly this young, agile couple cannot be married. He is an Adonis, she, a young version of Gwyneth Paltrow, perfectly made up. They've been running every day, both of them, in that incredibly springy way, totally effortlessly, in unison.

He always wears the tightest spandex shorts. Let's get a tape measure and clasp it around his buff rear just to see what a guy's perfect rear measures. Hers is hidden behind a fortress, a long tee shirt that reaches down mid-thigh. They bounce and talk easily, rarely acknowledging me. Her light laughter pervades the path like a lovely perfume.

But a few months ago they stopped running. Was he transferred? Was she? Did they have a mammoth fight? Did they simply drift apart? Recently she was running with a female, a sure sign of a break up. A woman friend is helping her pick up the pieces.

Then one day they were running again, as though they'd never stopped. The twin impalas. If they marry, will the lovely banter disappear? Will the sweet, bouncy jog give way to grim determination to get the exercise done for the day? Will they run alone to gain some freedom? How long will it take for the airy banter to dry up? The batteries to wear out? The novelty of running together to fall flat? And then I think of the 80-year-old couple and my faith in relationship longevity is restored.

"Stars and Stripes Forever" pops up next on my Sony Walkman. I continue on, filling up my strawberry basket with each exhalation.

Houses Should Be Forever

The other day a friend and I chatted about our former lives as Connecticut residents. I said, "I really miss my old house." She answered, "Oh, poo. It's only a house."

Only a house? She herself had never lived in a house for longer than 10 years, so I'll forgive her. But when we sold our house we sold 23 years of life and it was traumatic. What that house had seen. What it had lived through. Tears and joy. Two babies were born and grew up. It had seen teenagers' heartaches and heartthrobs, endings and beginnings. So I decided to write my friend a letter — one of those letters you write but never send.

Dear Irene,

When I walked my mother through an assisted living center years ago, the social worker listened as Mother made the expected comments. "I don't know about moving here. I really love my home and my view."

"Well," said the social worker, "You can't hug your home and your home can't hug you, but you will find people here whom you will want to hug and who will hug you back."

I am a person who believes stuffed animals have souls. I'd no more abuse a teddy bear or stuffed dog than a human being. So perhaps it is understandable that I feel a house is a living, breathing being.

"I remember, I remember the house where I was born," is the start of a poem Mother recited to me many times. She knew it as a child. Houses were important to her.

I remember when I was planning a Christmas dinner for 17 relatives. A week prior to the 25th, my husband and I discovered we had rats in the not-so-finished basement, which is where I was planning on serving the meal. The exterminators described the rodents as "Norway rats — as big as bear cubs." That's what they said.

My kindergarten-age daughter had told me for a week, "Mommy, someone was banging on the door in the basement last night. I heard it again this morning. I was too scared to get out of bed to tell you." I soothed her and dismissed it. And then realized she'd heard the rats gnawing through the basement door.

I remember when my daughter was very young and was sick and needed medicine. "Tweet, tweet. Feed me like a little birdie, Mommy," she'd say, opening her tiny mouth. She feeds her own babies medicine now. She had mono once, right after a trip to the Caribbean, and all she wanted was virgin pina coladas.

When she was 16 she met her husband-to-be. I'd peek at the two of them from my top-floor bedroom window as they sat in garden chairs working hard to get a tan. And we all love to remember her adventure as a beginning driver. Learning to drive a stick shift, she mowed down, with machine-gun precision, a couple of hemlocks that lined the driveway.

I remember my son Jay's birthday, when he had just turned two. The first guest arrived and rang the doorbell, and Jay was at the top of the stairs, wearing a pair of brand-new shoes. In his excitement somehow he managed to trip and fall all the way down the stairs.

I remember teaching him the names of coins, as we lay on the carpet on the front hall. I can remember exactly how he looked in his Cub Scout uniform. I can see his teenage bedroom and I'm pretty proud of myself that I let him keep it the way he wanted it, with the mattress on the floor.

I remember another time when my 15-year-old son walked in the front door having spent the weekend on Cape Cod with a buddy, sporting a highly visible hickey on his neck. It was somewhat of a badge of honor and symbol of adulthood.

Remembering... what a beautiful concept. It's not the house I miss. It's just the times gone by in that house... The way things were... What used to be... "It's only a house?" I don't think so, Irene.

Dad, Me, And The Canaries

When Peter, the canary, started his morning solo, Mama and I simultaneously screamed at him, "SHUT UUUUP!" We'd look at each other and collapse, giggling. Peter saw fit to sing when Sibby, "the middle sister," played Chopin's "Butterfly Prelude." Also known as "the sensitive one," Sibby thought Peter's ear-splitting singing was the bird's attempt to drown out her playing.

Peter was the last of a long line of canaries my father reared. The express purpose of these birds (it seemed to me) was to destroy the kitchen radio sounds of Fats Domino, Elvis, or the Everley Brothers. My sisters and I gave the birds the respect we thought they deserved, namely, none. They were Dad's toys. We had more lofty

169

things to busy ourselves with --- me, make-up techniques and fashion magazines, my sisters, homework. (It's a joy to be the youngest.)

Peter was a roller canary, a descendant of birds raised by people in Germany named Hartz, who lived in the Hartz Mountains. The Hartz people bred these birds over a period of 400 years. Singly, each bird lived its life in a closed room, paired with a master singer who taught it a set of trills and melodies. Peter's forte was an earsplitting roller coaster noise that would have been wonderful for drowning out my children's heavy metal stuff in the mid-seventies. But he was gone by then. Flown off to birdie paradise to drown out faulty notes on angels' harps.

Recently Mother reminisced that Dad raised 32 canaries before I was born, then slowly lost interest in them, though one or two always hung around. Several years passed before he bought Peter. Dad named him Peter because that would have been my name, had I been a boy.

***

When I moved to Florida, I wanted a canary, but none of the pet stores had one I liked. I never imagined owning two, but at a bird fair at the Morocco Temple, I saw a pair of American Songbirds owned by a bird fancier who raised birds at home. She said canaries are out of vogue, having been displaced by parrots and cockatiels. "People don't like the mess the birds make flinging their food all over their cage and the floor," she said. (Reverse marketing technique?)

I was barely listening. I'd fallen in love with two gorgeous birds. It seemed unfair to separate the Tang-colored one from its companion, the color of a White Russian and Tang combined. I would soon be getting great stretching exercises, bending over with a dustpan and whiskbroom.

Driving home, I was stunned at how human they seemed, as they sat in a cage, which I'd placed on the passenger seat beside me. They checked me out as they swayed back and forth on their swing. They cocked their heads at me, and the male echoed me when I "peeped" at him. I found myself talking to Dad, something I hadn't done since he died. *"Look, Daddy. Isn't this hilarious? I never paid attention to your birds. Now I've bought two. Can you believe it?"*

Arriving home with the dainty birds, I was sure I'd face the jealous wrath of my 15-year-old poodle, but after a flurry of annoyance, Amos, a little deaf, settled into bored understanding that the creatures were not leaving.

Later that afternoon, to transfer the birds to their larger cage, I enlisted the help of two friends — she, a nurse, he, a Mayo doctor. I figured they could resuscitate me if I passed out as the birds escaped and flew up into my 15-

foot ceilings or into a ceiling fan, splattering my birds to the winds before I could even introduce them to my husband.

The cage-to-cage transfer took half an hour. I named my birds Lovey and Dovey, just to annoy my grown children, which it certainly did. I settled their cage onto a little table in the breakfast room, so they could look at the St. Augustine grass and appreciate the palm trees and my neighbors' sawgrass and pittisporum.

The birds adapted to their new surroundings instantly. *(Intelligence is measured by one's ease of adaptability.)* They ravenously nibbled at anything. Romaine. Bananas. Strawberries. Carrots. And Dovey's personal favorite, broccoli. Lovey would barrel past Dovey to get to the day's apple slice and bark out a complaint if her male friend "bully-beaked" his way past her. I have never eaten more healthily in my life. Too bad I couldn't get the birds — especially Dovey — psyched about Dove bars.

Dovey stretched out his indignant self at her whenever she'd hog the Song Restorer treats, as though to say, "HEY! Those are mine. I'M the one who sings." While he made a beeline for the fresh, nonfat stuff, she pigged out on the more caloric commercial seed foods. Dovey was trim. Whenever I'd put a new, foreign food, such as a grape, in their dish, she wouldn't touch it until he taste-tested it first.

Their daily routine was amazing. The second after I put out their food, Lovey, the female, would get to the birdseed fast. Always took her bath before Dovey. Always took an afternoon nap. Always liked to have the cage covered by dusk and then she'd tuck her head into her tangerine feathers.

I hated to miss watching them take their bath. I was late to volunteer jobs, haircut appointments, and church so I could watch their antics. Lovey always won the race to the little plastic tub, pecking at the water several times — to test the temperature? Satisfied, my "five-pound" canary plopped her whole tonnage in the bathtub, displacing half the water and flapping her wings until the water doused my plantation shutters. With only an inch of water left, Dovey took his tub, a far less invigorating soak. He was a businessman with a train to catch. When Dovey was done, the two of them rested on their perch, side by side, the same way they slept. Après bath, thoroughly soaked, they looked pathetic and skinny without their grand ruffles of feathers.

The owner's response to my query of, "Does he sing?" was, "Oh yes, he sings to the female all day." But when I brought him home he did not sing for weeks, though he did chirp at Lovey. I was resigned to hearing only his chirp for 15 years. On the other hand, maybe he was molting. When birds lose all their feathers, a textbook explained, they feel unhappy *because they have no reason to sing!* At any rate, on the 4th of July, Dovey opened his beak and sang the long trills and melodies I'd been hoping for. *"Listen to that, Daddy! He's singing!"*

It was a melodious, gentle sound and Sam didn't mind when Dovey sang along with his flute, though I wondered if a "Shut UUUUp" wasn't around the corner. If we had friends over, I'd insist they arrive at Show Time, 3:00 P.M., when Lovey awoke from her nap and Dovey presented his afternoon aria. His morning song was almost unending. I should have a neighborhood coffee.

My children both live up north, and whenever they'd call, I'd say, "Listen to this." They'd listen. "Wasn't that spectacular, you guys?" They'd groan. "This is long distance, Ma." I gave them blow-by-blow accounts about how the birdies were kissing and how they were building a nest. I expected my kids to say, "Enough with the birds, Ma. Get a life!" How much could my children take of my yapping about a honey-and-nut food stick from PetSmart? How spellbinding can something be that can't be patted. Pretty spellbinding.

Several years ago, after my daughter was married, I was visiting a friend. We said our goodbyes and as I was leaving, she said, "Please do give my love to the love birds!"

"I will," I said. "They spend their days either eating, sleeping, or bickering." When she looked at me with blank horror, I realized she was talking about my daughter and her husband.

The two birds are gone now. Someday I'll probably get an itch to start all over again. Because of them, I talk to Dad a lot more and hope he's listening from a place where there are loads of birds, maybe even Lovey and Dovey. *Sorry, Dad, I should have paid them, and you, more attention.*

Call Me Grammie

I remember it as though it were yesterday. Wistfully, my husband said, "Is that all there is?" I had served him a small bowl of cut-up lettuce and tomatoes and a tiny sliver of quiche. I had warmed up a hearty bowl of New England clam chowder, his favorite, and then forgot to give it to him. I found the sad, Saran-covered soup in the microwave the next day. How can you forget to serve your tall, skinny husband part of his meal? It's easy. Because your daughter's having a baby. Another one, in fact.

Another thing I forgot: I wrote a letter of thanks to a dear friend and somehow it got swept up in a Christmas card envelope addressed to my sister in Seattle. I have lost checks. I have lost tomatoes. I call friends to ask them things they've already told me. But it doesn't bother me if people think I'm coming down with senility. I know better. I walk around with ginger ale in my veins — champagne, come to think of it — and feel like celebrating. I've learned to savor these delicious days because the days of magic are upon me. Magical days help you survive the tough days, the ones we all have. You tough it out, you wait it out, letting your good memories help you through. I am storing up my todays. *My daughter's having a baby!*

Last night, with a hard freeze about to knock out many plants on our north Florida property, I did remember to cover my huge potted bird-of-paradise plants. Being from seriously wintry Connecticut, I feel Floridians simply play at winter. I felt like playing in the snow last night, but there was no snow. I covered the plants with king-sized sheets so they'd look like January snow ghosts. When I walked the dog around 10:00 P.M., he behaved like a scaredy-cat, alternating between barking at the sheets and shying away from them. I hated to hurt his feelings, but I had to laugh.

I alternate between having bursts of energy and being suddenly exhausted, needing a nap. I am deliriously happy. I am focused on one thing. Nothing else matters.

The other day I went to a pet store that allows shoppers to play with puppies. I lifted up the wee pups, patting them on my shoulder as though to burp them, and swaying to and fro, back and forth. I chose puppies that felt similar to the weight and length of a newborn infant. I need to retrain. To practice.

I am expecting a second grandchild and am poised to have Sam receive another telephone call like the early morning one that jolted me out of the shower two years ago. The call from Connecticut came three weeks earlier than expected. "Sam! Tell Mom my water broke!" I was 1,100 miles away *and shampooing my hair*. I flew north fast and arrived half an hour before she gave birth. This time, she's in Tampa. I'm only 300 miles away and taking very quick showers.

My daughter and I are soul mates and I feel somewhat guilty. I don't have the back pains, the cramping, the pre-labor contractions, the big belly, nor the upcoming labor. I have all the fun, none of the work. Around Christmas, my son-in-law told me if I wanted to I could be in the labor room with them. All I could think of to say was, "No, thanks. Joseph's mother-in-law wasn't at the inn." Besides, my job is to play with the new baby's big sister. I am stocking up on crayons, paints, and, to my disbelief, CD-ROMs. I hope I've mastered them. They're geared for toddlers.

I am unable to concentrate on my prime love, reading. Books are unloved and untouched, not even catching my attention on the nightstand. The few book reviews I have written are on small, non-complex books; my critique is on a par with an eighth grader's. The editor called me today. "Did you mean to say 'grandmother's house' or 'mother's' in paragraph two?" Oops.

I lost my car registration yesterday, drew doodles on my score of Rutter's *Requiem* at rehearsal, and was late picking someone up at the airport. "Miss Organization City," as my children call me, is in a happy coo-coo land. Or perhaps in a cocoon. And the baby is not due for two or three weeks.

What will the newbie (as we call her) be like? Will she love *Teletubbies* and *Blue's Clues* like her 23-month-old sister? Will she eventually play by herself in her crib for a good hour after a nap? Will she sleep 18 hours a day for her first six months?

At a year and a half, will she love to swing on a trapeze at gymnastics? And love even more the rubber stamps that the teacher will put on the tops of her tiny feet at the end of class? Will she worship her Daddy and demand that only he wind up her musical dollie at night? Her

Mommy says, dead serious, but with arched eyebrows for our benefit, "Oh yes, Mackenzie, I understand. Only Daddy can wind up dollie the right way."

I wonder if the new baby will giggle when I dump buckets of water unceremoniously on her head to rinse off the shampoo. Will she refuse to hold my grown-up hand in a supermarket parking lot and insist on eating at the table standing up? Will she "read" an illustrated children's encyclopedia with me and say, "Wow!" at the illustrations when I do? Maybe she, too, will do somersaults in her crib when I open her door first thing in the morning. Maybe she will also open my closet and point to my nightgown, the one with Tigger on it, and say, "TIGGARR! TIGGARR!"

Will she cry her tiny heart out and fall to pieces when I kiss her goodbye at the airport, sobbing out the car window as I walk to the gate, "'Ammie! 'Ammie!"?

One thing I know: I will continue to watch in wonderment as my daughter, my own baby girl, continues to experiment with her own particular way of mothering. I will marvel at the way she loves her own cubs with complete, selfless abandon. A love so primal, so deep, so fierce that I need to step back and wonder where this comes from. People say being a grandmother is wonderful, but nobody told me about this private, unfolding, ongoing joy. I wonder if someday I will remember this as though it were yesterday.

Life With "The Legend"

Mother started signing her letters "The Legend" when she was 85. None of us, her three daughters, was particularly surprised. One of the definitions of "legend" is "an unproved story." Mother always told stories about her life. We were not sure what was true and what wasn't. But we *were* sure she was not Anastasia, the missing czarina.

"Legend" also means "a person who is very well liked in some areas." "Legend" is the perfect word for this lady who is now 94. As she always said, "Mama is ALWAYS right."

God forbid I should call her "Mom." She'd say with disgust, "'Mom' sounds so common." I never could figure out what was so bad about "Mom." Common sounded kind of nice to me, kind of normal. We three sisters had no trouble calling her "Mummy." NEVER "Mommy." (Too common.) Later, when it seemed a bit odd for college students to be calling one's mother "Mummy," we switched to "Ma." It is only now that she is officially Mother. When you're 94 "Mother" seems fitting. She has not protested. But she hasn't protested lately when I test the waters and call her "Mom," either.

Her favorite name was "Maw." It had a down-on-the-farm, we-all-ride-in-rodeos sound to it. She fancied herself to be alternately a bullfighter and a cowboy. Trail rides were her favorite. She, my Dad, and middle sister signed up for the wilds of Idaho or other western states that seemed like Africa to me. To my oldest sister and me, anything west of New York was a little too uncivilized.

But though Maw was at home on the range — riding by day, spending nights around a campsite, and collapsing into sleeping bags at night — her other persona was one of glamour. She loved to dress up. To me, she was playing at dress up, in a ball gown, on her way off to a dinner-dance.

***

Because of Mother, I thought the whole world came to a standstill during summer afternoons so everyone could read. She read to me until her throat was raw — she often told me it ached — and by the time I was able to read on my own, I read whatever books popped into view.

In the earlier grades when I came home from school a kid or two would stop by and ring the doorbell. I usually begged Mother to tell them to run along and play while I read a chapter or two. She tried to persuade me to go outdoors with them. The other day, when I called her at her nursing home, she volunteered, "You always *did* love to read," when I asked her if I could send her any books.

She awakened in me a lifelong fascination with the czars of Russia, and, to this day, I cannot walk by a bookstore without checking for a new book on Nicholas and Alexandra. Mother was, of course, Anastasia. "I can remember being tossed in the gutter to die, and being taken to the hospital in the depths of winter. The nurses didn't believe me, so I escaped ..."

And on and on she'd go, fabricating immense lies. Why? Conversation is more fun, she reasoned. As a child I was spellbound. As adults we found her untruths confusing or infuriating. My older sisters were spared these tall tales when they were children. They were brought up by an assortment of nannies. But when I was born, perhaps to assuage her guilt at wanting a boy so badly, she raised me herself.

Until I was old enough to go to school, she began the day with coffee and *The New York Times* on a tray in her bed. Then we ate together in my room, at a tiny table, pretending to be two imaginary people, Mrs. Merital and Mrs. Latimer. "Mrs. Merital is, of course, Mrs. Latimer backwards, you realize," she announced one day. Well, sort of.

The menu remained the same: coffee, a bowl of Cheerios with a dollop of always-strawberry jam, more coffee for her, hot chocolate for me, and, the quintessential breakfast finale, a hot croissant, with a slit

183

in the side for a melting Droste chocolate. When we finished, she'd read *Les Malheurs de Sophie* to me, switching from French into English so easily that no one could tell she was translating as she went along.

Food was an important part of our lives. We were trying to make up for those "starving Armenians" in Europe. That sobriquet gave Mother the vapors. We were to say, if asked, "We are of Armenian extraction." We were NEVER to say we were simply "Armenian." It was OK to say we were "of Armenian descent." But I liked the extraction word, as though our family had all been pulled out at birth by some bizarre, disoriented dentist.

I do believe a sweet tooth must involve a gene, in my case, Mother's. But this tooth was cultivated also by a beloved Polish cook, Mary Wizack, who had a French cooking background.

And if Mary's cooking wasn't rich enough, there were little Viennese patisseries that Mother and I frequented. They magically appeared no matter which street led us homeward to our New York apartment. You entered the stores by climbing down five or six steps to enter. Climbing up to leave wasn't enough to work off the calories, but we were not counting calories in the 1940s. I kept up nicely with Mother as we ate lacy cookies and Viennese tortes.

Mother introduced me to a restaurant called The Three Crowns. It was a true Swedish smorgasbord, in the days when restaurant buffets were rare. Once, I asked Mother if we could go to "The Greek Hounds." It took her a while to realize I meant The Three Crowns.

Life stopped on Tuesday nights when Sid Caesar and Imogene Coca came on our black-and-white TV. When the reruns of *I Love Lucy* first came on the air, we'd sit by a blazing fire in winter and watch the morning shows when I should have been in school. "I have a sore throat. I better stay home today," I'd say, putting on my sick face, knowing it would get me an enormous supply of comic books when Mother came back from a trip to Larchmont's village. I was good at drumming up a sore throat if I thought about it hard enough.

For lunch, she'd bring me grilled cheese sandwiches and cherry pie, wonderful for a sore throat. I was set for an afternoon of radio soaps. Around 5:00 o' clock. I'd debate whether I dared get away with another day of being home to watch *Lucy* and read comics and fan magazines. I was pretty sure Ma would love the company.

A Sample A Day
Keeps The Doctor Away

Going to the grocery store is, to me, like a trip to Disneyland — a glorious treat. And if I haven't shopped in a few days, I get itchy. I need a fix. I need to sample the honey-roasted peanuts, the angel food cake drizzled with orange goo, the cubes of ham speared by a pretzel rod.

Grocery shopping in the 1950s was a horrid chore, as boring as a trip to a paint store. A grocery store was a meat-and-potatoes thing. Aisles of meat, potatoes, and boring cans of veggies and fruits, soups, fresh stuff, and a couple of choices of soda pop. I suppose cookies were sold, but calories started to matter in the 1950s, and Mother dashed me past anything that smacked of dessert. Too fattening. When the sugar-free cola No-Cal appeared on the shelves it was a miracle. I was allowed to drink all I wanted — chocolate, root beer, orange.

Things picked up when Grand Union began selling Swanson's TV Dinners. Now Mother could have a second Manhattan, and I could take a tray to the sunroom and revel in fried chicken, mashed potatoes with gravy, and peas. It felt like a regular dinner, instead of mother's forte, a single hamburger, no bun, no dessert. Eventually TV dinners came with dessert. Nirvana.

Today, I am amazed at the goodies one can sample at banks, automotive service centers, and so on. I can't wait till my car needs to be serviced because the homemade cookies and chocolate-dipped macaroons, arranged on lacey, paper doilies, are out of this world. And at my bank? Forget the drive-up window on Fridays. If I go inside to make a transaction on Fridays, I can get a cup of coffee and oatmeal or sugar cookies. *(Get inside girl! There are cookies to be had!)* At Christmas, the tellers bring in homemade treats in the shape of Santa or Rudolph.

At Harris Teeter near the deli section there's a tray that holds three kinds of chocolate cakes and pies in sample cups. Nobody's overseeing my consumption, so that must mean the store wants me to sample all of them. I'd never starve if I were homeless. I'd just go where the food is.

I'll bet I've consumed 1200 calories just driving around doing morning chores. That leaves me with only a few hundred calories for the rest of the day. Now in the afternoon, if I go to Costco, the wholesale store, I'll run into Dixie cups of lasagna. Bagels with cream cheese. Mini slices of pizza. On opening day there was so much to sample, I went around in a food coma for 48 hours. Not long after that, the Post Office was celebrating some milestone and handed out decent-sized squares of cake. Never saw that happen in the 1950s.

At Christmas I discovered a nearby store that sells pricey gift items and leaves open containers of chocolate-covered pretzels and cookies for sampling. Or you can taste a variety of dips on crackers. They're so good I've debated wearing dark glasses, putting on a change of clothes, and going back for more.

The thing is, I don't have well-developed taste buds. I don't get my jollies out of duck en brochette or beef Wellington. Which is probably why I'm perfectly happy waltzing around Jacksonville getting my calories from stores here and there, hoping the mega-vitamins I downed with my morning eggs are doing sit-ups in my body.

At the end of a long day doing quality control checks on all this food, I'm ready to eat something more nourishing (and serious) than Peterbrooke's chocolate-covered popcorn. More likely than not, this serious food turns out to be a beef (or chicken or turkey) patty.

I'm glad Mom taught me how to cook a hamburger. But I'm also happy my car only has a few hundred miles left before its next service check. You have no idea how delicious those homemade cookies are.

Lost In Manhattan

Gale and I were best friends by default. We both went to Rye Country Day School but lived in the village of Larchmont, New York, about half an hour away by car. Our 15 classmates all lived in Rye, so we had no other nearby pals, from third grade to grade twelve. We took the train to RCDS for many years, a 45-minute trip each way that involved taking a bus from home, then walking up a steep hill to school. It was a novelty for a while but tedious during downpours and snowstorms.

Gale was fascinated by the things my parents allowed me to do. We couldn't have been more opposite when we met at age eight. For one thing, she called her parents by their first names, which was and is incomprehensible to me. For another, grades *had* to be the most important thing in her life. From third grade on, her mother made it clear that Gale would go to her mother's alma mater, Smith College.

Gale was not allowed to use the kitchen toaster or steak knives until she was almost a teenager because her parents felt they were too dangerous. She was an only child. I was the third of three. By the time I rolled in, my parents let me decide how I behaved and when and if I studied. My grades were solid. Rock bottom. In the root cellar except for English. Gale was always on the Honor Roll. I thought she should be happy, but she often called me shrieking and sobbing over some injustice, some punishment at home. It was frightening to me.

In her first year at Smith, Gale had a hard time handling the freedom and her grades reflected that. I was at a different college, and we drifted apart so I stopped hearing about any volcanic phone conversations between Gale and her Mom or Dad.

***

In seventh grade all that mattered to Gale and me was that finally — complete miracle — our mothers decided we were old enough to go by train without supervision to see a Saturday matinee on Broadway. My mother worked for weeks to get Gale's mother to agree. Finally, after Gale pleaded interminably, Mother Marge agreed.

Mother was opposed to Gale's parents' keeping such tight reins on their child. When Gale and I were caught doing something naughty, Gale's mother became enraged. The screaming matches Gale and Mrs. R. jointly threw in plain view of the two of us regularly appalled Mother.

My mother just took a deep drag on her Lucky Strike and said to me, "Don't do that again. OK darling?" Sometimes Mom and I playacted to show them How to Parent. "OK, Mama, I'll be good." See? This is how

190

mothers and daughters should behave, we were telling them.

Though Mother didn't cotton to Marge, my mom was happy to take Gale and me to New York plays when we were quite young, third grade or so. And Gale's mother would quickly reciprocate. Back in the 1950s Broadway plays only cost $5 a person. We were joyously reaping the benefits of our mothers' games of tit for tat, so we saw many musicals. Our favorite pastime was to choreograph, dance, and sing to *Plain and Fancy, The Music Man, My Fair Lady, The Pajama Game* and dozens of others. We knew all the lyrics by heart.

***

It must have been late spring of 1957 when we waved goodbye to our mothers and climbed aboard a train bound for the big city. It wasn't "The Big Apple" in those days. In a cloud of my mother's Arpege, I bustled onto the train steps, followed by Gale, suffocating in her mother's Chanel No. 5. Gale was terrified, so I had to be the one to give off vibrations of "There's nothing to it. I was born in New York, for heaven's sake. I know my way around." Bravado was in my coat pocket.

The day was perfect. Spring was budding everywhere. We had been given enough money to take a taxi over to Broadway, have lunch, see the play, and catch a cab back to Grand Central in time to hop on the 5:25 to Larchmont, where we'd be picked up. But it didn't work that way.

The play was exhilarating — I can't remember what it was. We probably would have thought a musical of *Humpty Dumpty* was fabulous. When we left the theater I said to Gale, "We don't need to take a taxi. Why not walk? I can get us to the station." After all, the theater was in the forties, and Grand Central Station is on 42nd Street. I was giddy with the power, the freedom. So, like a teenage prequel to Thelma and Louise, we took off on our little adventure. We had plenty of time to catch the train. Of course we did.

Well, of course, we didn't. I managed to lead us as far west as one can go in Manhattan, instead of going east, to Grand Central. Past Broadway we walked, past 8th Avenue, 9th Avenue, 10th ... Suddenly, we stopped raving about the play. Instead of a sea of matinee-goers, bustling on their way somewhere, there were few people.

We could smell dinner wafting from the tenement buildings and finally started racing in the opposite direction. We had long since missed the 5:25.

5:30 ... 5:45 ... 6:00. We didn't want to waste time calling home. Besides, it was long distance.

Taxis were hard to find. Our new "high" heels were killing us and we were getting hungry. Should we use our cab money and eat hot dogs instead? Eventually, we found a cab.

On the train ride home, Gale and I were much less talkative than on our city-bound train. We pulled into the Larchmont station around 7:30 P.M. and watched our mothers peer into each window as the train slowed into the train station. My mother's face looked taut with concern as she stood waiting with Mrs. R. I dreaded listening to Gale's mom's torrents of wrath and wondered if my mother would say, "Don't do that again, darling."

Not quite.

Casual At Sea? No Casualty

My husband will never be President of the United
States. He can't stand to watch more than the first five
minutes of any Presidential convention, so I doubt he
aspires to hanging out at The White House for four years.
But if he ran and won, forget the economy, the Middle
East, health care — his attire would give him the biggest
headache.

Decades ago when Sam was striving to start his own insurance agency, he arose at 6:00 A.M., and put on a tie and jacket. He did not take them off for 35 years. Finally he was done with knocking on doors to sell insurance, going to corporations, and dealing with applicants for secretarial jobs who abused the King's English: "My brother, he be's a night watchman." Another applicant, equally grammatically challenged, asked about the name of the agency. "C&R? Does that stand for courteous and reliability?" It was an unparalleled attempt at humor, so to speak.

When Sam retired, he announced he'd retire all but one tie and one business suit. Except for honoring the dead at funerals and my daughter at her wedding, he does not get dressed up. Years ago his jacket had a gig, a one-night stand, on the Norway's Caribbean Cruise for Jazz Lovers.

Which brings me to the sticky problem that arose a month ago: we had signed up to go on another cruise. Meaning there would be the traditional formal night and he'd have to wear a dinner jacket (no way), a suit (no way), or at the very least a jacket (OK, a jacket.)

He surprised me by asking, "Want to pack for me?" He'd always loathed the thought of my packing for him. I eagerly — no, "anxiously" is the right word — accepted. "Will five tee shirts be enough?" I asked. He agreed. "Three shorts OK?" "No," he said. "One is plenty, my khaki ones."

What else went into the luggage? One bathing suit, pajamas, a couple of pairs of underwear, and a few sundries. He also capitulated, grumbling, to the necessary jacket and slacks for the one formal night. This is not traveling light, this is traveling *lite*.

***

Cruising has changed. In my mother's day, valises were stuffed. On a week's cruise every night was formal except for Costume Night when people came in garb brought from home or had fashioned impromptu, with help from the room stewards, surely not their favorite task. Passengers would go dressed as fruit bowls, animals, celebrities, Roman emperors in togas … and there was always an old geezer who dressed as an infant, wearing a bonnet and a cloth diaper and carrying a baby bottle. Today's cruise lines have gotten the message: people want it simple. Really simple. There's only one formal evening on a seven-day Caribbean cruise, and the rest of the time you wear resort casual.

***

Our first night aboard ship was Sunday, and Monday we were at sea all day jogging around the seventh deck four times, which equaled a mile, sampling cooking classes, learning How to Beautify Your Face (me) and How to Win at Blackjack (him). Midday, Sam discovered his only pair of shorts had a huge stain on the rear end but it didn't bother him.

By 6:00 o' clock we were dressed for dinner and ready to check out the caviar, the salmon mousse, the baked Alaska. But ... *my goodness, these people certainly look dressed up,* I thought, as we snaked through the ship to the "eating salon." From our cabin to the Seven Seas Dining Room on the Norwegian Majesty was no small distance.

More and more, we saw dinner jackets and fancy long gowns floating by us. No one was dressed as we were, in our Ponte Vedra Casuals. How silly, I thought. Don't these people realize the ship tells people in *The Cruise News* when it's a night for formal wear?

Whoops! We just hadn't read it. When we got to the dining room, the maitre d' greeted us as though nothing was wrong, and we swept our way in as though everyone else was dressed inappropriately. He seated us near the front of the room, a great view. We could watch people enter in their finery. One other couple similarly dressed was seated with us, but we were the only four passengers out of 1600 who wore the wrong clothes. Sam was in heaven. His jacket snoozed in our cabin closet for the whole cruise.

A Bell Is A Wish Your Heart Makes

December 6, 1992. I sit in the church van next to people I've known for 12 rehearsals and realize a thick band of sweat is creeping down my neck, threatening to saturate my white silk blouse.

I'd driven to Disney World before, but always with excitement, not fear. On this day, I refuse to let my fellow passengers know about my throbbing insides, my spinning stomach, my headaches ... all week long. I want to tell them I am scared and sick, scared sick, but telling them will make it real. How can the land of Mickey and Goofy be causing me such panic? HEY! I'm going to Disney World! So how come I feel like throwing up?

***

Working at a K-12 school for four years I had enjoyed listening to the children play handbells. It looked easy. The sound was delicious. I told myself, "I can do that." Someone said, "If the stars could sing, their sound would be like a handbell choir."

My job at school ended in August, and my husband and I drove 18 hours straight to our new home in Florida, arriving on Saturday night, exhausted. The next morning, I treated myself to a lazy half-hour of reading the Sunday paper before unpacking the stacks of boxes. There in the paper was the announcement I'd been hoping to see. A handbell rehearsal at the Methodist Church in Jax Beach would start at 5:00 P.M. on that very day. It was on my agenda to find such a choir; I just didn't think it would be THAT soon. I unpacked all day long, showered, and drove to the church.

I wanted so much to make music with a team of musicians again. The excitement of singing in school and later in community choruses never left me and I wanted to recapture the joy. There was only one problem: in my safe choir haven in the alto section, my sight-reading ability had been good or bad in direct relation to the persons singing on either side of me. If I heard a particular line of music once, my musical ear could pick it up. Handbells would be a new challenge.

Even after years of piano lessons, I don't read music well. I'd always wait until my teacher played a piece, then I could mimic it. Easy Chopin, Bach, a little Scarlatti, Scriabin. In choir, I always angled myself so the strongest singers were right behind me. I'd hear something a few times and have it more-or-less memorized. In a rehearsal, you can fake it if you lose your place and you can mouth the words momentarily. With the words as your guide, you aren't lost for endless measures. But in a handbell choir, you are the only one playing particular notes. Nobody plays them but you. There's an ugly vacuum if you're responsible for the D-sharp above middle C and you've lost your place

On the eve of age 50, life was fantastic. The worries of child rearing were gone, as was the quest to be a size eight. My plan was to cultivate a love for "everything Florida" in our new home state. Meeting new Floridians, especially musicians, was part of my settling-in plan. I also wanted a new challenge. But after a certain age, can you learn to play an instrument?

The beginners' bell choir was easy because the director had circled the notes. Notes circled in red were for the one handbell, blue for the other. What a brilliant idea! I'd more than muddled through; I'd held my own. I felt energized enough to unpack another batch of boxes that night.

To my amazement the next day Mary Ruth, the director, called to ask if I wanted to rehearse with the advanced group that plays at Disney each Christmas. Two evenings later I rehearsed with them. The sounds coming from the other ringers were magical. My own sounds were not. Feeling like I'd gotten an F in music, I drove all the way home after rehearsal in the pitch darkness, forgetting to turn on the car headlights. We had rehearsed "Jingle Bell Jazz" and rich arrangements of joyful Christmas medleys, some with complicated, syncopated rhythms. I wasn't so sure I could play these.

For weeks I muddled through. I debated bailing out after every rehearsal. How could Mary Ruth have asked me to play with the advanced group?

***

The Disney concert was approaching and by mid-November I was panicky. By Thanksgiving my heart pounded all day long before the evening rehearsals. I could play well enough if Mary Ruth counted out the measures, but I knew she wouldn't do that during a performance. Sometimes I was so lost the music swam all over the page. I'd lose many measures until she'd call out, "Measure 135!" We were practicing eight or more songs, some of which were five, six, even 12 pages long. Standing there looking and feeling stupid, trying to find your place was agony. And you can't raise your hand in a performance and ask, "Where are we?" Mickey and Goofy would hold their bellies and chuckle at me in our upcoming concert at the U.S. Pavilion at Epcot.

I tried to count out the beats in each measure, but I was so nervous I'd count six beats too many, or eight too few. I'd think we were on measure 14 and we were really on six. Or vice versa! Mary Ruth clapped out a particular rhythm in a phrase, and I had no idea when I was to come in. Instead of being able to relax and listen, my mind froze. You can't learn anything when you freeze up.

Maybe you can't learn anything after a certain age. Maybe I'm too old for this. I kept taping our rehearsals and listening to them all week long. Driving. Sleeping. Cooking. Walking the dog. I brought my music home and picked out notes on the piano, sometimes working at it for two hours a day. Sometimes again for an hour after *Jeopardy*. I refused to tell Mary Ruth how panicky I was.

I missed a rehearsal in October because of a trip to Aruba but sat on the beach and listened to my practice tapes. The surf was ... an annoyance!

Despite my anxiety, I did survive my first nighttime Christmas concert at Disney and only missed a note or two. My fear must have been transparent because when we stopped around midnight at a restaurant on our long drive back to Jax Beach, someone leaned over to me and said, "It does get easier." I guess she figured green isn't my normal color. From that time on, I felt bonded with the other musicians..

***

I played for five years and looked forward to performing in church on Sundays, especially at our huge Christmas concert. We played at weddings, at the Grand Floridian at Disney World, and at Epcot's Christmas Candle Lighting Service. Practicing, week after week, I stopped losing my concentration, but if I did occasionally, I slid back into place. Far from being petrified, I began to relax and loved sharing the incredible, glorious music. I wanted to tell the audience, "Wait till you hear this. You won't believe someone could have written anything this beautiful." I could actually hear the music when I stopped being so nervous.

I had to end my handbell "career" several years ago because I've inherited Mother's disease: Arthur visits me — I have arthritis and my thumb joints are messed up. I learned on the bigger, heavier bells that keep the rhythm and which are, to me, more fun. I've been told I would surely need surgery if I continue to play. Do I mind not playing any more? Not a bit. I had my day in the sun.

***

Growing up, you expect to learn new things. You take it for granted. But learning new stuff after you reach a certain age ... that is magic.

Slow, Slow, Quick, Quick, Slow!
Oh God, Not DANCING SCHOOL!
Say It Isn't So!

From September 1954 to June 1957, starting in fourth grade, I was forced to go to the Meekers Ballroom Dancing School. The classes were held in Rye Country Day School's auditorium every Friday of the school year. If I could have made a giant leap from the 3:17 P.M. bell at school on Friday to Saturday morning, I would have been ecstatic. But alas, the gods were on Fred and Ginger's side.

The Friday afternoon school bell was not liberating. I had to go home. Take a bath. Get into a party dress, a velvet or satin deal my grandmother sewed, which fit when she measured me, but squashed me to death at the final fitting. Mother fed me a dinner of dollhouse-sized peas and a tablespoon of hamburger so I'd have less of a belly to suck in as I whirled around the auditorium, yanked around by (and sometimes having to yank around) a sweaty, equally reluctant partner.

TGIF? Thank God it's Friday? Humbug. But Saturday? Saturday was heaven. Saturday meant escape to the magic of the Larchmont Movie House, to watch Esther Williams swim as I planned to swim someday, to listen to Debbie Reynolds sing as I surely would soon, and to study Elizabeth Taylor's acting as I would act one day. I would be a combination of all three women! At the very least, I was Broadway Bound. What an outrage that I was stuck with the sweaty palms and clumsy feet of boys who also ached to be anywhere but at a ballroom dance class.

Either Mama or my friend Gale's mom drove us from our homes in Larchmont to Rye, where we danced for one hour. Once in a while, Mama or Gale's mother took us to Nielson's ice cream parlor, where Gale gorged on an ice cream soda and I devoured a hot fudge sundae until we both had raging stomachaches but wouldn't admit it. The most ridiculous thing was that our mothers thought dancing school would help us get skinny.

Most of the other girls spent forever combing their interminable blond locks before going to stand in the receiving line. We all had to curtsey to the hostesses as the band played. As we lined up, the other girls picked apart some of the boys but swooned over most of them.

For the last two years of the Meekers class we became cool and made a point of talking about how much we hated it all the way up in the car, hoping to drive our moms crazy. It didn't. From November to April we prayed a gigantic snowstorm would blitz Westchester County and that our mothers would conclude it was too dangerous to risk the half-hour trek up U. S. 1.

For me a Friday night snowstorm meant spending a delicious evening wrapped up in a warm bathrobe, hibernating. An uninterrupted night of TV; Sebastian, my beloved dachshund; comic books. Eventually we discovered our mothers loathed driving us in the dark, but they were convinced the discipline of learning to dance was too important for us to skip.

One Friday, I was so desperate to stay home, I did the old trick of taking a thermometer, putting it on a light bulb, and hoping it would climb to a worrisome fever. I held it to the bulb too long, and the tip broke off. I was too honest to ditch it in the back of the medicine cabinet, so I confessed what I'd done. That night, I danced.

And again, the next Friday rolled around too soon, and I had to miss *The Mickey Mouse Club*. I was so envious of Annette. Poor Annette, Mouseketeer supreme, today she is a victim of Multiple Sclerosis. Neither of us dances any more. Despite my every attempt not to learn to dance years ago, I can do a respectable waltz, fox trot, cha cha, meringue, lindy, and tango. Trouble is, nobody asks me.

Recently there was a brief sighting of John Travolta at the Ponte Vedra Club. If he returns, I will be happy to dance with him ... as long as he doesn't have sweaty palms or talk about sports.

Two Precious Gifts:
When Jay Met Melissa

"It's going to be a breech delivery and you're ready to deliver soon. Would you like to have your baby today?" The doctor's words were magic. The due date was three weeks away. I thought, "And give up having the mini acrobat use me as a trampoline? YES!"

It was March 1, 1971. March graced the garden with bouquets of crocuses and azaleas. It would be the birthday of my second child. A glorious day. The beginnings of a New England spring, and the last traces of snow, gone.

I hastened home to settle my two-year-old son, Jay, with my mother-in-law. "Jay, when I come home, we can read to the baby. It's going to be fun to have a brother or sister, isn't it?" My jolly old pregnant self beamed positive messages, hoping he wouldn't misbehave to get me away from the newborn. I handed him a fire truck wrapped in Sesame Street paper. It was an instant hit. So far so good.

I arrived at the hospital at 1:00 P.M. My husband ate cheeseburgers. I salivated. We played gin rummy and a pathetic game of Scrabble, marveling that our scores could descend to such incredible depths. We watched soap operas with one eye and batted names back and forth again. I became cranky.

Finally, the doctor appeared at 6:00 P.M., and out popped Melissa at 6:16 P.M. People with lengthy labors hate me for this. And such a civilized hour. Dinnertime.

The next three days were heavenly, Melissa and I alone together. My little girl. My little girl. I kept saying those three magical words over and over. My mother called her "The Rosebud." How lucky to have a swaggering buckaroo, and now a daughter. We named her Melissa Anne.

How Jay would react to a new little person in the house nagged at me. Had I told him *"Now you'll have a friend to play with"* too much? Who was I kidding? Jay would want to pitch a tent in the back yard and have her as his tent mate ... tomorrow. I wondered if I'd have to worry about my newborn treasure being battered by his new toy fire truck.

Typical two-year-old bruiser, Jay liked to hurl himself out of his crib at first light and run giggling into our bedroom. It didn't seem funny as I lay in the hospital, thinking if he could do that, he could go into Melissa's room and ... do what to her?

On going-home day, a raging gale blew ice chips at my hospital window. Snow would soon smother the azaleas.

My husband was delayed an hour. His mother waited at our home, sitting with Jay. When we came up through the garage, I said to my husband, "You carry in the baby." I wanted my hands free to hug Jay.

A fire crackled in the living room fireplace. "Hey, Jay! Come downstairs," I said. He peeked around the banister, wearing his pajamas with the mini dragons. He seemed unusually quiet. "Come see your baby sister." We had her in a navy baby carrier made of canvas. I put her down on the sofa so Jay could take his first peek at Melissa. He seemed indifferent.

He stared at her, then dashed upstairs. My heart sank. We stood, feeling awkward, listening to the clock ticking on the mantelpiece. Before I could plan what to do next, Jay came bumbling down the stairs with his red-and-white checkered quilt. He raced into the living room, then stopped and walked on tiptoe to the baby's side. He patted his treasured security quilt around her, tucking her in with a velvet touch. "'Zaaa's blanket," he whispered. Jay's quilt was now Melissa's, and he'd given her her first nickname, too.

Twenty-five years later, Jay's "little baby sister" became engaged. He fretted about what to buy the couple for a wedding present. He had to hurry; the wedding was only a week away. Then it suddenly came to him. The perfect gift: a quilt for their bed.

Peripheral Neuropathy:
Can This Disease Be Stomped Out?

(This article ran in *The Neuropathy News* in December 2001.)

It is 6:45 A.M. in Ponte Vedra Beach, a barrier island in north Florida, my home. A good time for a morning walk. Tropical plants brush my legs as I walk along the pathway on this roasting day in August. The resident alligator is taking a sunbath near the lake. Walkers, bikers, runners nod to me and pass by swiftly. Jerry, a neighbor, tips his cap and pounds past, running on Cypress Bridge Drive South in the opposite direction. "Hey, how are ya? Ya got that serious walk today!" I smile, say hi, and think, *You're*

damn right, Jerry. Yes, I've got that serious walk. I am pounding my feet into the concrete. I am angry with them.

During the course of the day if I try to rest with my feet up, it feels as though electrical currents are coursing through each foot, or that my toes are plugged into an electrical outlet. At night it often feels as though a thousand ants are all wiggling to get free. Sometimes my feet pulsate or feel as though they're shriveling, drying up. Sometimes they are numb, other times, they are fireballs, ready to explode, or like the worst imaginable sunburn.

I have a condition called Peripheral Neuropathy, which means in its simplest definition, usually irreversible damage to the peripheral nerve endings. Early on I didn't know about the irreversible part. I just thought it was a temporary thing — as in, it's no big deal; it'll soon stop.

I look down at my feet and alternate between barking at them. "Are you out of your mind behaving like that? Quit it, you brats!" And mollycoddling them, cheerleading: "It could be worse, little piggies. Get better!"

If you look at my feet they don't look abnormal. No bruising. No bleeding. No swelling. It feels as though they're double their normal size. *I must be wearing a thick sock or shoe,* I tell myself when I lie in bed, and then I remember — no, it's the Neuropathy. People have been known to climb into bed with their shoes on because they can't tell if they're on or off. Sometimes I think my eight-pound poodle, Charlie, is lying on my feet and I try to whoosh him off the bed — but no, he's by the window, dreaming of conquering alligators.

One Day in January

My "little problem" started in January of 1996, right after my 52nd birthday. I can divide my life into two parts: before PN, and after. My husband and I drove, sun roof open, jazz blaring, to a new mall in Georgia. It was a chilly, sunny Sunday, the type of winter day Floridian transplants call "the reason we moved to Florida." I found a store that sold deck shoes and bought a pair, the first ones I'd ever owned. I wore them for a couple of weeks. My feet burned and tingled. *Phooey. I'm allergic to the shoes' lining.* I threw them in the back of my closet. The tingling, burning continued.

I bought a small whirlpool bath for the feet, which turned into a drinking bowl for the dog. Because my nerve endings had gone haywire, moderately cold water made my feet feel as though they were freezing. Hot water was out of the question — it made my soles burn even more. Tepid water? Useless.

About a month later, my shoes were driving me wild. To ease the burning, I wore socks with flats or sandals. Not a pretty fashion statement. Putting on the softest socks was like pulling sandpaper along the soles of my feet. In bed I

213

couldn't bear the weight of a sheet or blanket. Best was (and is) the cool wood floors of my home. But not ceramic tile. Brrr! Too cold. It's a variation on the story of the three bears: too hot, too cold, just right.

Many weeks later, I went to my internist. My deck shoes were not the problem. She suspected Neuropathy. Because she knew one third of Neuropathy sufferers have diabetes, she checked me for that, but the results were negative. I was lucky that diabetes was not the problem, but also lucky that she even considered the possibility of Neuropathy. Many people go to doctor after doctor before they are correctly diagnosed. She told me to see a neurologist. I was dumbfounded. No one in my family had needed one.

Surely there's a pill somewhere...

Reluctantly, I did make an appointment with a neurologist, still thinking I should let time pass and the problem would fade, like a bad muscle ache. *"He'll give me a pill and I'll be rid of this thing."* On my way to see him, even with the a/c blasting, it felt as though a furnace was raging near the pedals. When I put my fingers near my calves to "feel the heat" my hand felt only the cool air. *"If I tell the doctor this, he'll think 'this woman is a nut case'."*

The neurologist ordered tests including an EMG — electromyography — to measure the electrical properties of the nerves. The results were negative, proving I didn't have certain diseases. But those early tests didn't prove I did or did not have Neuropathy either. The doctor suggested I had some kind of sensory Neuropathy and implied there was nothing he could do. "I'm sorry about your pain," he said, even though I'd told him I could not describe what I had as pain. "Pain," I said, "is childbirth. This is not childbirth."

Later on, I would learn about the tests one can have, some simple, such as pin pricking, for example, that could reveal numbness. Other more invasive tests might indicate a loss of sensation, loss of balance. More sophisticated tests might point out why you have PN. Or they might not, meaning your problem is idiopathic, which somebody said sounds like a combination of idiot and pathetic, but simply means "cause unknown."

Who ever heard of such a weird disease?

I started devouring information about Peripheral Neuropathy and found more than 132 reasons why a person can have Neuropathy, such charmers as Lyme disease, thyroid problems, alcoholism, AIDS, cancer, rheumatoid arthritis, kidney disease, even leprosy. I asked every doctor I came in contact with about Neuropathy. A podiatrist said he sees five or six people each week who complain of the same problem. What a complicated disease! One person's symptoms may be entirely different from another's. And symptoms change day to day.

The annoyance escalated and finally in January of '99, I discovered a website, www.neuropathy.org. It led me to a doctor who is a leading specialist of the disease in New York City. (This was before I discovered a local specialist in Jacksonville.) Because I visit the Northeast often, I made an appointment with him at Columbia Presbyterian Hospital. He found I had numbness, loss of sensation, and loss of balance. After taking 16 vials of blood and doing quantitative sensory testing (QST), he determined that my Neuropathy's etiology is idiopathic.

The doctor prescribed Neurontin, which is, nowadays, often used for Neuropathy sufferers. It is a drug whose label use is to help epileptics, a fact that I found bizarre and scary. Today, I just feel ... hey, whatever works. The pills do lessen the symptoms.

I learned that The Neuropathy Association has estimated more than twenty million people in the United States may have the disease. Some don't know they have it because they're in the early stages. The condition is, in most instances, not life threatening, but many people must go on disability because of the chronic pain.

I became used to blank stares from friends when I described the symptoms, as in, *"What are you talking about?"* They asked, "If your feet are numb, how can you

216

feel the burning, stabbing, and so on?" I told them my feet are like the United States. There can be a blizzard in Boston, sunshine in Miami, and torrential rains in Seattle.

My lifeline was, and is, *The Neuropathy News*. People with Peripheral Neuropathy write to the newsletter saying, "The pain is so bad I haven't slept for six months." "Driving is scary." "My 13-year-old daughter has it." "Pineapple has helped me." The website points readers in the direction of a "cure" in another country (Norway) or state (Arizona) and it doesn't seem like such a bad idea. We are all tilting at windmills.

Toughing it out is not the way to go

It is understandable that some people think we're exaggerating. *("Oh yes, I know. My feet get hot too.")* Or that they think excess weight is the culprit. (We have lots of skinny members in our support group, thank you very much.) But it is *not* understandable that doctors are so poorly educated about it. *"You have to live with it,"* a respected internist in Stamford, CT, told me only a few years ago. *"Just forget about it,"* he said. As it turns out, forgetting about it is the worst thing you can do. Shame on all of these doctors! It's a bad idea to use the tough-it-out philosophy. The longer you wait to seek help, the harder it is to control.

Eventually you **do** have to get on with life, but you need to establish a baseline and get medication to calm things down, if possible. Many people experiment with lotions and soothing creams or dietary supplements until they find something to help them. Hunting around for the perfect seamless socks or best moisture creams is a lot better than moping. I have a drawer full of this 'n that — stuff that did not work for me, but some things do help for a couple of weeks. Then I'm on the hunt for something else that might work for a while.

The hardest thing about Peripheral Neuropathy is trying to explain it to loved ones. My daughter and I had quiet, blissful moments together after her first child was born. But now my *three* granddaughters are five, three, and almost one, and I'm not able to jump around and play the way I want to. The Neurontin saps my energy. It is joyous to monkey with them at a park, though I pay for it with a flare-up at night. The sheer delight of playing takes my mind off the feet gremlins.

Someday a cure will come

It is 7:30 A.M. I've been walking for forty-five minutes to a tape of polka music. Tomorrow, parade music. Humidity exacerbates the Neuropathy problem and the sensations go up to my knees or thighs. Summers are difficult in Florida, but I've found when the humidity is

218

high up north, it can be brutal too. Florida is the lightning capital of the world. TV bombards us to take cover and crouch low if we feel a tingly, electrical sensation in our feet. I just laugh because the electricity is my nearly constant companion.

Summer or winter, walking helps. Does the energy boost give me a natural high? Probably. Does it help the circulation? Maybe. Do I feel better just doing something positive? Absolutely. But I never know how much I'll be able to do. Sometimes, by midday, this shopaholic can only walk at a mall for a short time. Other days, I can stay there as long as I want. I'm grateful my car has cruise control so my hands can do much of the accelerating and decelerating. Actually I'm grateful I don't have the many diseases that are mushrooming everywhere.

It's encouraging to read in the latest *Neuropathy News* that The Association has grown to more than 40,000 members and boasts 200 support groups. I dream about Barbara Walters or Katie Couric doing a TV special on Peripheral Neuropathy.

A magic pill is out there. I know it is. But for now, the best symptom-relieving "pills" for many people are the little support groups, some with as few as six members in remote places, that chug along month after month, gathering steam, gathering passengers, and spreading the word about Peripheral Neuropathy. If you don't have a support group in your area, start one. Write to The Neuropathy Association, 60 East 42nd Street, Suite 942, New York, NY 10165. Or call 1-800-247-6968. They'll jump-start you onto the right track.

Stop Crummy Days!

What are your ways of coping with days when you're in the dumps? E-mail Mims Cushing with your ideas at mims1@attbi.com. Or write to her c/o The Neuropathy Association, 60 East 42 Street, Suite 942, New York, New York 10165.

And/Or...

If you enjoy writing short, personal stories (humorous or reflective) send or e-mail those as well. We're considering a second book ...*Son of Crummy Days!* This one would include your stories. Stories must be typed and cannot be returned or acknowledged.

The Neuropathy Association,
60 East 42nd Street, Suite 942, NYC, NY 10165
www. neuropathy.org   1-800-247-6968

If you have received a free copy of this book from a friend and would like
to send a check for $10 to The Neuropathy Association, please send it to
the address above. No sales tax required. Any additional donations will be
most appreciated.

If you live in the Jacksonville area and would like to pick up your book locally, e-mail
mims1@attbi.com for information.

Ordering Books By Mail

Please PRINT the following information. You need not use this form

Name_____

Address_____

City, State & Zip_____

Telephone Number _____E-Mail_____

I am enclosing $10.00 per book, plus shipping & handling:
$2.00 for the first book, $1.00 for each additional book.
Outside the U.S.: $4 and $2.

Total $_____

Send your order to:

The Neuropathy Association
"Brush Off the Crumbs"
60 East 42nd Street Suite 942
New York, New York 10165

The Neuropathy Association,
60 East 42nd Street, Suite 942, NYC, NY 10165
www. neuropathy.org   1-800-247-6968

If you have received a free copy of this book from a friend and would like
to send a check for $10 to The Neuropathy Association, please send it to
the address above. No sales tax required. Any additional donations will be
most appreciated.

If you live in the Jacksonville area and would like to pick up your book locally, e-mail
mims1@attbi.com for information.

Ordering Books By Mail

Please PRINT the following information. You need not use this form

Name_____

Address_____

City, State & Zip_____

Telephone Number _____E-Mail_____

I am enclosing $10.00 per book, plus shipping & handling:
$2.00 for the first book, $1.00 for each additional book.
Outside the U.S.: $4 and $2.

Total $_____

Send your order to:

The Neuropathy Association
"Brush Off the Crumbs"
60 East 42nd Street Suite 942
New York, New York 10165